ALL THE TEA IN CHINA

ALL THE TEA IN CHINA

How to Buy, Sell, and
Make Money on the Mainland

JEREMY HAFT

Founder and Chairman of BChinaB Inc.

PORTFOLIO

PORTFOLIO

Published by the Penguin Group

Penguin Group (USA) Inc., 375 Hudson Street, New York, New York 10014, U.S.A. • Penguin Group (Canada), 90 Eglinton Avenue East, Suite 700, Toronto, Ontario, Canada M4P 2Y3 (a division of Pearson Penguin Canada Inc.) • Penguin Books Ltd, 80 Strand, London WC2R 0RL, England • Penguin Ireland, 25 St. Stephen's Green, Dublin 2, Ireland (a division of Penguin Books Ltd) • Penguin Books Australia Ltd, 250 Camberwell Road, Camberwell, Victoria 3124, Australia (a division of Pearson Australia Group Pty Ltd) • Penguin Books India Pvt Ltd, 11 Community Centre, Panchsheel Park, New Delhi – 110 017, India • Penguin Group (NZ), 67 Apollo Drive, Rosedale, North Shore 0745, Auckland, New Zealand (a division of Pearson New Zealand Ltd.) • Penguin Books (South Africa) (Pty) Ltd, 24 Sturdee Avenue, Rosebank, Johannesburg 2196, South Africa

Penguin Books Ltd, Registered Offices: 80 Strand, London WC2R 0RL, England

First published in 2007 by Portfolio, a member of Penguin Group (USA) Inc.

10 9 8 7 6 5 4 3 2 1

LIBRARY OF CONGRESS CATALOGING IN PUBLICATION DATA

Haft, Jeremy, date.
    All the tea in China : how to buy, sell, and make money on the mainland / Jeremy Haft.
        p. cm.
    Includes index.
    ISBN 978-1-59184-159-3
    1. United States—Commerce—China. 2. China—Commerce—United States.
    3. International business enterprises—China. 4. Investments, American—China. I. Title.
HF3128.H34 2007
382.0973'051—dc22   2006052756

Printed in the United States of America
Designed by Carla Bolte • Set in Dante
Graphs by John Del Gaizo

For Alma

CONTENTS

1 GETTING STARTED   1
What do you think, my name is Fink!

2 READING THE MARKET   17
The world is still round. (And why that's good.)

3 ORIENTING YOURSELF   37
Deng's Law of Uncertainty: "One never knows, do one?"

4 BUYING FROM CHINA   65
There are four of us—me, your big feet, and you.

5 SELLING TO CHINA   109
The best revenge on a lousy customer is to sell him more goods.

6 COMPETING WITH CHINA   157
Close the doors, they're coming through the windows!

Afterword: SEEING THE FUTURE   187
From Beijing to Boca Raton

Acknowledgments   193
Notes   195
Index   199

ALL THE TEA IN CHINA

1
GETTING STARTED

What do you think, my name is Fink!

The head hunger striker from the Tiananmen Square uprising is glomming another plate of stone crabs. It's his third.

Now he's flinging half-eaten claws like mahjong tiles onto a growing discard pile. Those leavings might have fed him for a week when he was on the barricades in Beijing. But this is Miami Beach—and our dissident-from-the-Chinese-backwoods-turned-entrepreneur is in sheer heaven. If launching a new business on the mainland means raising money in South Florida, then he could get used to capitalism quickly.

People mistake him for the bookworm who stood in front of the tank in Tiananmen Square. He's not. To the movement's leadership, that guy was a nobody, a foot soldier who vanished—as Tiananmen's A list trod more illustrious paths.

Some went to jail. Many went into business. Some went to jail, *then* went into business. They racked up MBAs and JDs from Yale and Columbia; cavorted with billionaires at Davos and Aspen; then went back to China to start companies.

Is this the biggest sellout in modern history?

Actually, it isn't. Making money had nothing to do with their intentions. Waging revolution did. And by trading their prison stripes for pinstripes, the dissident entrepreneurs of Tiananmen showed us a

completely new way to achieve sweeping political, social, and economic reform in China—without standing in front of tanks.

But for the rest of us (who are more concerned with paying the
kids' tuitions than with shepherding the fate of a billion people), they
showed us that you don't have to be General Electric to trade with
China. They showed us that businesses of all sizes can capitalize on a
once-in-a-century windfall opportunity to make money, build value,
and create jobs.

China is undergoing the largest and most rapid middle-class expansion since the rise of the United States, Western Europe, and Japan. Its
middle class *today* already outnumbers the combined populations of
the United Kingdom and France. These new consumers need modern
products and services—but China can't provide them; its technology
and capabilities remain decades behind the West. The United States,
then, is uniquely positioned to provide the many products and services
China's vast and growing consumer base needs.

This phenomenon is already playing out. China is America's fastest
growing *export* market—and has been for a decade. Since 2001, in fact,
U.S. exports of goods and services to China have grown *five times faster*
than to the rest of the world.[1] Some export categories, like cotton, are
even growing in triple digits. Plastics, pulp, power generation and
medical equipment, industrial machinery, and many other U.S. exports
to China are surging by 30 to 40 percent a year.[2]

Who knew? Savvy companies, that's who. Sales from American
firms to China have more than tripled in the last decade.* But the best
news of all is that small businesses—not just the large multinationals—
are cashing in. Exports to China from small and medium-sized enterprises (SMEs) have been ranked the largest gainers in the world for a
decade.[3]

So while the shelves of your local Wal-Mart may teem with Chinese

*For more charts, visit AllTheT.com/charts.

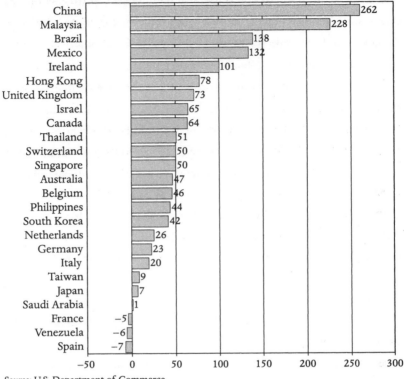

1992–2002 Percentage Changes in Exports by SMEs to Top 25 U.S. Markets

China	262
Malaysia	228
Brazil	138
Mexico	132
Ireland	101
Hong Kong	78
United Kingdom	73
Israel	65
Canada	64
Thailand	51
Switzerland	50
Singapore	50
Australia	47
Belgium	46
Philippines	44
South Korea	42
Netherlands	26
Germany	23
Italy	20
Taiwan	9
Japan	7
Saudi Arabia	1
France	−5
Venezuela	−6
Spain	−7

Source: U.S. Department of Commerce.

merchandise, China is actually buying goods and services from the United States at a much faster clip than we are from them—giving many U.S. industries a big boost.

As exports to China boom, imports become more dynamic. Savvy U.S. firms today are thinking way beyond just "outsourcing." They're importing goods from China to extend core business lines, enter new U.S. markets, and defend low price points from China. That's right: many U.S. firms are importing Chinese goods to parry Chinese competition. And some firms, like auto parts manufacturers, are exploiting two-way trade: exporting products to China to expand sales, while importing from China to protect markets at home—and all the while, creating jobs locally.

But this is just gravy. The meat, my new partner insists, is that by doing business with China, we help guide the most populous country on earth into becoming the kind of modern nation that is good for the West—a peaceful, stable ally and trading partner.

I squint at the enigma across the table. His face is flecked with shards of shell and meat. Stone crabs, he declares, are now his official all-time-favorite food. (At $55 a pound, I should certainly hope so.)

He sets in again. With the sharp crack of each new claw, I start to hear a cash register jingle in my head: Crack . . . *ka-ching!* Crack . . . *ka-ching!*

He eats like a buyer, my grandfather used to say—like a hungry client who happily pigs out on your dime. But I'm buying what he's selling. The upside in China, he insists, is huge and real. China's economy has already quadrupled in size.[4] It will double again in the coming years. We can get a piece of that action.

He fingers another crab shell. It's 1999. A decade anniversary of the uprising just passed. Everywhere, the headlines are touting China's meteoric growth. We haven't a clue what kind of business we'll launch on the mainland, but we know we're headed for the right market.

We'll need seed capital. (Crack . . . *ka-ching!*) We mull over friends and family we can put the bite on. The pickings are lush in the land of real estate developers and dermatologists. I smile when I imagine the hard-nosed Chinese dissident pitching woo to a breakfast club of Miami retirees.

He's got the face of a man who's cheated death more than once. His right eyelid sags languidly. It cuts his big, black iris in half and makes his gaze look gimlet and hard. A tough cookie, no question. Yet he's as bubbly as Dean Martin on his third martini. (I would learn that many of the dissident entrepreneurs of Tiananmen are the same.

Their battle-scarred exteriors have been burnished by Ivy League class-rooms and Wall Street boardrooms.)

A true entrepreneur, he's also seen failure. He snuck into China after the crackdown and risked arrest to launch two dogs. One venture was aimed at servicing China's nascent Internet sector, the other, legal services. Both deals tanked.

Yet he's stammering with excitement to tell me why he wants another go at it. Why, after trying to tear down the Great Wall, the dissident entrepreneurs of Tiananmen are rushing back to scaffold it. Why he, who risked his life to revolt against China, would risk his life again to trade with it.

Well, for one thing, China's problems are big and dire and could derail the economy. But that's not the whole story. Certainly, he loves his country and wants to try to help, but he also loves America. (He'll go on to become a U.S. citizen.) He wants to see both countries benefit.

To fulfill these twin goals, he points out a basic congruence: China's enormous challenges are the West's market opportunities. To redress one, you enrich the other. Both parties benefit. To explain why, though, he must return for a moment to first cases: the uprising itself.

Wait a sec, I've heard about these Tiananmen guys. They gave marathon lectures about Chinese history and ethics to the troops deployed in the square. As the seminar begins, I can see why the soldiers got sore. Nobody likes a pedant.

CHINA'S CHALLENGES
ARE THE WEST'S MARKET OPPORTUNITIES

He leans in. For starters, the uprising at Tiananmen had about as much to do with democracy as the Boston Tea Party had with caffeinated beverages. The movement's original purpose was to stop government corruption—not to push for free and fair elections. Democracy got grafted on much later.

Stopping corruption? How banal. Yet this aim was more revolution-ary, more *visionary* than a desperate adventure to overthrow the gov-ernment. The originators of the uprising understood that until corruption was licked, democracy was the least of their worries. Modernity itself was at stake.

The Tiananmen leaders were no dummies. These were the top ninety-ninth percentile of China's university students—in a country where getting into college is based solely on academic performance and has nothing to do with your extracurricular activities. (China's fa-vorite extracurricular activity is not football. It's doing your home-work.)

Brainiacs from all over China—not just Beijing U.—converged on the square. Their Paul Revere? The Internet. The uprising at Tianan-men Square was the first successful use of the Internet to mobilize great numbers of people. Before Meetup.com, which revolutionized American electoral politics by Internet-powering the right to free as-sembly, before there even was a World Wide Web, Chinese universities were networked, employing secure computer linkups to share data. Some of the technically savvy among Tiananmen's leadership under-stood the power of this network to enlist supporters and disseminate information across the vast country. They used crude electronic bul-letin board systems to put the word out on the street.

Eggheads far and wide heeded the call. In the middle of the big square, with the portrait of Mao looming over them, they scurried into cliques as if it were the first day of grade school. Yet Tiananmen was a popularity contest among China's university elite. Scientists, his-torians, journalists, mathematicians: they were in line to take over top positions in government, industry, and academia. Why would these young superstars choose to risk it all—their careers, their very lives—for a cause like stopping corruption?

Because they knew their history and feared for the future. In 1989, it seemed everything was on the line. The Chinese people had endured seven hundred years of war, famines, and servitude—concluded by a most vicious coda, the twentieth century, which they dub "the Century of Shame." In that time alone, they endured a grisly civil war, wholesale cruelty under Japanese occupation, and Mao's regime, which felled tens of millions of men, women, and children through famine and violence.

In America, each succeeding generation expects to do better than its forebears—indeed, usually feels entitled to do so. Imagine looking back over a hundred generations of suffering and premature death in your family, your city, your nation. And suddenly, there's a ray of hope.

On the eve of the Tiananmen Square uprising, an unstoppable steamroller of progress seemed to be plowing over all the old ways. Picture the Industrial Revolution and the fall of the Berlin Wall happening at the same time. The old, agrarian command economy was rapidly being eviscerated by a modern, industrial marketplace. At the same time, the Communist regime was transforming itself, experimenting with more liberal forms of governance.

Deng Xiaoping, Mao's successor, ratified a constitution in 1982 that employed the concept of rights as an organizing principle. The "rule of man" had governed China for many centuries, so the adoption of a constitution based on the concept of "rule of law," and the rights of individuals, was a radical departure from the past.

Yet corruption and fraud had infested every aspect of civil life— from government to military to industry. The constitution and its laws were a sham. Municipal and provincial governments were rackets that extorted money from citizens and companies by fiat. An independent judiciary was nonexistent. Banks and businesses were run by a league of cronies with their hands in one another's pockets. They gave money away to each other to prop up the dying state-owned industry sector, while denying loans to the private sector.

Corruption was putrefying the new economy, killing true competition and innovation. If corruption was not brought to heel, the leaders at Tiananmen feared China would fail to achieve modernity, and another century of shame would be to come.

The leaders pressed not for regime change but for institutional change: the adoption of the rule of law, honest civil and corporate governance, and an independent judiciary. These institutions, they believed, would not only support China's evolution into a modern prosperous state, at peace with its neighbors, but would also provide the underpinnings for a more open, liberal society.

Many in the government were sympathetic to the demonstrators' arguments. For some time, it seemed the students might actually wring some concessions from the authorities. But a dangerous game of chicken ensued, and the People's Liberation Army (PLA) had the last word.

The leaders who were not rounded up or killed made daring escapes, aided primarily by the French and the British. One escape featured a dramatic dash by sea: a dozen identical speedboats fanned out from the harbor in Guangzhou, breasting the waves for Hong Kong. They were all decoys, save one, which stowed the runaways. Chinese security gave chase. Shots volleyed in the air. The leader made safe harbor in Hong Kong and was spirited away to France, where the Mitterrand family personally administered hospitality.

President George H. W. Bush, who was an ambassador to China from 1974 to 1976 before we officially began fielding ambassadors there, resisted intense public pressure at home to demonize China. This former chief of the U.S. Liaison Office in China did not overtly aid in the leaders' escape. China's crackdown on the demonstrators had consequences—just not ones that would cause China to lose face at the hands of the Americans on the global stage. Instead, Congress enacted an embargo on all weapons sales to China and pressed Europe to do the same. This U.S.–EU embargo remains in force, twenty-five years after the crackdown, despite some recent maneuverings by the Europeans to have the ban lifted.

The leaders at Tiananmen regrouped in the West and continued to meet, argue, and plot their future plans to wage revolution. Standing in front of tanks was pointless. Sure, it made the evening news, but it didn't change the basic conditions in China.

So to press their mission to build honest civil institutions, they began employing multiple modes of attack: through conducting trade, through lobbying China policy in the West, and through participating in nongovernmental organizations (NGOs) inside and outside China. Rather than isolating and penalizing it, they sought to bring about reform by working with China—through the rules-based economic and regulatory systems to which it now belonged, and on which it so dearly relies for its continued growth and stability.

China needs all the help it can get. Its challenges are mind-boggling in their enormity and complexity. Geography, demography, political economy: each presents big difficulties.

Consider geography. China is a vast country, yet much of its land is uninhabitable. Half of China's 1.3 billion people, therefore, must live on land the size of Texas. To make matters worse, the deserts are claiming more and more of this habitable land every year.[5]

Demographically, China must now contend with the consequences of its birth-planning policies, which were put in place by Deng to rein in the runaway growth of the most populous nation on the earth. Three generations of birth planning have created the "one-two-four" problem: one adult child must support two parents and four grandparents. That puts a tremendous burden on the state and small families to pay for the aging population. The laws and policies are therefore evolving. Multiple children are often encouraged in the countryside and permitted (for a fee) in the cities. But as China is loosening population controls, it continues to struggle to provide its people enough water, food, and energy.

Aside from geography and demography, China faces a doozy with its political economy. It must move a billion people from an agrarian to an industrial system—as quickly as possible. As a frame of reference, when the United States moved almost 70 million people from rural farms to factories in the cities, the migration took one hundred years and exacted a tremendous societal cost.

China must create twelve million new jobs each year for the next decade just to keep pace with new entrants to the labor pool created by population growth.[6] And it must figure out how to provide jobs for the millions and millions of its unemployed citizens. China's stated unemployment rate is 4.3 percent, which is equivalent to the entire U.S. labor pool being out of work. And there is a giant migrant worker population—estimated at 150 million—with no job security, no long-term housing, and no health care.[7]

It is easy to consign these conditions to the effects of Schumpeter's "creative destruction": old systems must die as new ones emerge. But try telling that to a worker whose "iron rice bowl" has just been shattered—one of the many millions who have lost their jobs in the dying state-owned industry sector.

Civil unrest, not surprisingly, is rippling through China's industrial cities and the countryside, with 87,000 reported cases (which means the actual number is higher) in 2005.[8] The Chinese are taking to the streets to demand stable jobs, good health care, and freedom from local corruption, which persists in undermining the new economy.

In short, China is walking a high wire with no net. Up until now, dollar-denominated trade and investment have ballasted the economy. With nearly one trillion dollars' worth of currency reserves, the government and banks have essentially been plowing free money into real estate and infrastructure development.

And that's causing problems. Investment in China's fixed assets grew 30 percent in 2005 and contributed a whopping 47 percent to China's GDP.[9] These easy credit policies have created more bad debts and fewer new jobs. Overcapacity in real estate and manufacturing is growing, and China's central bank has started raising interest rates, to prevent the economy from overheating.

To make matters worse, it's actually getting more expensive to buy growth, and that growth is becoming very wasteful. In the 1980s and '90s, it took two to three dollars of new investment to produce one dollar of additional growth. Now it takes more than four dollars.[10] Even India is more efficient by that measure.

If you read the Chinese media, you'd get a much better sense of the very earthly problems this "miracle economy" faces. Daily stories describe corruption, a debilitating health care crisis, severe environmental degradation, the growing divide between China's very rich and very poor, crime, and civil unrest, as well as a number of other factors that Chinese fear could derail their country.

In an uneasy alliance, Chinese leadership and the dissidents are working to...d the common goal of a modern, stable China. They are making amazing progress, given the magnitude of the problems. Economic development is having a profoundly positive impact on the poorest of China's poor.

UNICEF recently applauded China's success in combating child hunger, for example. While India has made only modest progress, and eastern and southern Africa barely any at all, China has already beaten the United Nations child hunger goals for 2015: to halve the world's percentage of underweight children and reduce the death rate for children under five by more than one-third. Wage rates are going up— usually by double digits per annum in the industrial cities—and the proportion of Chinese in poverty fell from 53 percent to just 8 percent between 1981 and 2001.[11]

China's environment is another problem of catastrophic proportions that is gradually improving. China's leadership recognizes the direness of the situation. It would be hard not to: China hosts sixteen of the twenty most polluted cities in the world.[12] It seems that every week, another glowing disgorgement of radioactive sludge spills into a river, and major cities downstream must scramble. For children in many cities, the simple act of breathing is equivalent to smoking two packs of cigarettes a day.[13]

Led by the proenvironment factions in the central government, China has adopted an aggressive energy policy that seeks to relegate oil and gas consumption to less than 15 percent of the total energy mix by 2020.[14] It is investing hundreds of billions of dollars into green technologies and green urban planning, while scouring the globe to import environmentally friendly products and services that will help in the cleanup effort.

As for labor conditions, Chinese workers are striking, rioting, and in many cases, taking their grievances to court. There are signs that the authorities are listening. They asked the public to comment in the spring of 2005 on a draft legislation to improve the rights of workers— and received more than 190,000 responses.

The law would impose stiff fines on companies that do not comply with antisweatshop rules.[15] And it grants additional powers to China's state-run union, the only union allowed to operate on the mainland: the right to establish worker rules, engage in collective bargaining, and pursue grievances. (Wal-Mart, though it permits no organized labor in the United States, was forced to unionize its China stores.) Although the law will most likely make doing business more expensive in China, it is a step toward improving labor conditions.

China is a work in progress. And it is *making* progress. But there's a lot more that still needs to be done. The dissident entrepreneurs of Tiananmen have blazed a trail for us to follow. Through doing business, they are helping to build civil institutions in China, while addressing some of the country's staggering challenges.

But here's the rub. The bigger the challenge, the bigger the market opportunity for the West. Take China's environmental crisis. Its industries, cities, and central government must import billions of dollars' worth of products and services from the West to address the problem. (A leading U.S. provider of environmental cleanup services, Duratek Inc. of Columbia, Maryland, is one forward-leaning firm trying to help.) China's mining safety? Power generation? Water treatment? Health care system? All are big challenges and all, big market opportunities.

And just as we can help redress China's woes, China can help redress ours, as well. To many battered industries, China presents hope. Take the auto industry. China is the fastest-growing auto market today. And though automotive production capability is improving in China, it still lags way behind U.S. technology and engineering. So China must continue to rely heavily on importing auto parts from the West.[16] While Detroit is in a tailspin, China's markets present a major opportunity for small and midsized U.S. auto part manufacturers to increase market share through export and in-country China sales. Steel is another industry that was bloodied a decade ago, but made a tremendous resurgence, in part because of the Chinese market.

Okay, okay. I think I get it. China's big challenges are big market opportunities for savvy companies. Both sides benefit. But I'm catching about every third word. Although my new partner holds two Ivy League degrees, his spoken English is difficult to decipher. My mind wanders.

There's a messy pile of crab shells between us. Stone crabs are a renewable resource, of sorts. Every season, they're culled from South Florida waters, and a single claw is clipped from each. The crabs are then chucked back into the drink, alive. Their claws grow back and are pried off next season. (And Sisyphus thought *he* had it bad.)

By 1999, waves and waves of American companies were already seeking their fortunes on the mainland, scuttling across the floors of silent seas—only to get their claws clipped off in China. Over and over and over again.

Little do we know, we're heading for the same fate. Even though we have a "China insider" on our team and lots of dough behind us, we'll still make mistake after mistake—sometimes putting the very viability of the business at risk.

I'm not alone. People who actually *are* doing business in China seldom have anything to report but horror stories. Real-life experience gives the lie to the rosy statistics. Whether they're China business veterans or first-timers, big multinationals or sole proprietorships, they'll just shake their heads and sigh.

Oh, China. We're working on that. A batch of PVC just outgassed chlorine and killed our lineman. Or, our joint venture partner moved in the middle of the night without a forwarding address. Or, we're trying to solve the mystery of how the goods arrived soaking wet inside a sealed shipping container.

The antics that go on in China make grown procurement agents cry. It's far and away one of the most complex business environments in the world. Yet those who are succeeding in China today are glad to have led with their chins, because they're making money, building value, and growing new market share.

Their success, I will come to understand, occurs not because they figured out the secret to unlocking some mythical pool of a billion customers. Or that they suddenly switched on a spigot of cheap labor. Both of these scenarios are illusions, and the road to Shanghai is littered with the carcasses of companies that chased after them and bit the dust.

Looking back on that day, and knowing what I know now, would I have stilled my partner's mayo-smeared hand? Avoided all that time, money, and heartache spent on false starts, missed opportunities, and wrong turns?

Perhaps. The missteps schooled me, but I see my journey in China as following a path that many have trod. The mistakes I made are the mistakes everyone makes. And they're *avoidable.*

Through the coming years I'd hear the same story over and over from clients. If a company did over a hundred million dollars in yearly sales, chances are, they'd already been to China and paid dearly for it in sunk costs. Large companies plowed their money into trial and error, building plants and hiring personnel. Middle-market companies plowed their money into trial and error, partnering and working with intermediaries.

If the firms were smaller, a great many of them were family-owned operations, and were in even worse shape. Margins eroding fast. Hating China and resisting going there—then suddenly feeling compelled to go and leaping at the first chance. And getting reamed.

Sitting there that day, I have no clue of the topography of pain I'm about to traverse. I look away from the crab shells and try my best to pose the toughest questions I can about pitfalls we might encounter, and what we'll do about them. To each of my questions, I get, "May guanti"—No problem—and that Cheshire cat smile. Who is this paradox? He is both dissident and collaborator, both altruist and profiteer.

I like him from the outset. But it's hard for me to reconcile the opposites. I can't read him. Punctuated by frequent breakdowns in comprehension, cognition, and judgment, our relationship will play out in miniature the same mistakes we'll make in the business.

I should have paid closer attention to a joke my dad used to tell me about a guy named Fink.

Fink owned a dry cleaning store, and in the window there was a big sign:

WHAT DO YOU THINK

MY NAME IS FINK

AND I PRESS PANTS FOR NOTHING

A man on the street sees the sign and runs home. He gathers all of his pants and brings them to Fink for pressing. A week later he picks up his order, and Fink hands him a bill for $25.

The man protests, "Wait a minute, Fink. Your sign says: 'What do you think, my name is Fink, and I press pants for nothing!' "

"No, sir," says Fink. "The sign reads: 'What do you think, my name is Fink, and I press pants for *nothing?!*' "

Fink is no fink. He's just bringing a different set of conventions to commerce. So are the Chinese. I will soon learn that to do business with someone you don't understand is to court disaster.

2

READING THE MARKET

The world is still round. (And why that's good.)

Our first trip to China begins with a plea for secrecy. Entrepreneurs or not, Tiananmen leaders are still enemies of the state. And those who publicly eschewed politics for commerce still had to make private deals with China's secret police before they could return. My partner was permitted to go back, but only after he'd had a couple sharp scrapes with the law. He was warned to be discreet, not to make a big deal of traveling in and out of China. I am told to follow suit.

I slink into the airport terminal. You never know who could be watching. Suddenly, there's a loud spasm of movement and color. It's my partner. I see a big straw hat. It has a wide flat brim the color of instant oatmeal. It flounces as he walks. Is that a price tag? I have gone into business with Minnie Pearl.

I'm thinking that this iconoclast might actually be trying to thumb his nose at the authorities. A ten-gallon hat and a yellow Hawaiian shirt that could guide tankers through a typhoon are what you wear when you want to attract attention, not deflect it—whether you're from Beijing or Boca Raton.

We shake hands and thump chests. He's grinning from ear to ear. He's tickled by the delicious irony that the Florida boy will soon be trodding on the ancient Middle Kingdom. He giggles to himself and shakes his head.

We are headed to Shanghai. From there, we'll take a bus to Ningbo. Ningbo is a port city that's thrived for seven thousand years. It sits across the Bay of Hangzhou from Shanghai. To fly, it takes about half an hour. To drive, you need to skirt the bay, one of the three largest in the world. That should take you about four to five hours, depending, of course, on what you encounter on the roads. They're building a bridge to connect Shanghai and Ningbo—the largest transocean bridge in the world, modeled in the shape of a flying dragon. When it's done, travel time between the two cities will be cut considerably, facilitating the flow of goods, capital, and people.

We arrive in Shanghai faster than I imagined possible. I'm shuffling from the gangway and am greeted by the strains of Patsy Cline's "Crazy" in the terminal. Times have changed. Driving from the airport, all we see are ads for American brands: KFC. Buick. Wal-Mart. The taxi driver does not recognize the name of the street we give him. He says it wasn't there yesterday. New streets are popping up every day.

To visit China is to feel like you're standing on the edge of the next millennium. You can smell change in the air. And you can see it all around you. Everything is in a state of becoming. Cranes crowd the skyline—the Chinese joke that the crane has become China's national bird—and jumpsuited workmen scurry up and down bamboo scaffolding fifty stories above the street. The old and new collide, as Shanghai's elegant Art Deco Bund (where 1920s expats and high rollers partied along the Huang Pu River) smacks up against a ridge of futuristic glass structures, breathtaking and bombastic in their modernity. You feel like E. B. White, looking out across the expanse of Manhattan in postwar America. The feeling of a muscular manifest destiny is palpable.

But in some ways, it's a grand misdirection. If you fix your eye on the moving object ("rising" China), it's easy to miss the forces that are propelling that object (integration into the world's economic system).

In misreading the dynamics of China's trajectory, we ignore the larger context, and market opportunity.

Let's give credit where credit is due. China's economic growth has been not a star turn but a team effort. Massive capital inflows of trade and investment from the West have propped up infrastructure and industries, created millions of jobs, raised wages and living standards, and fueled the largest middle-class expansion since the United States, Western Europe, and Japan.

That awesome construction boom you see before you, then, is actually being funded from cash reserves China has accumulated doing business with the West for twenty-five years. "China's rise," therefore, is somewhat of a misnomer. It implies that China is the animating force behind its own expansion. Rather, trade with the West and with its Asian neighbors has propelled China into superstar economy status, the only country in the world to overtake the United States in foreign direct investment.[1]

China's open markets have helped considerably, to be sure. As markets opened, capital followed. Today, China is one of the most open markets in the world. Trade makes up 80 percent of its gross domestic product.[2] Considering it was closed tightly until the late 1970s, that aperture is stunning.

This new openness derives, in part, from China's membership in the World Trade Organization (WTO). To join, China had to enact or change over 1,100 laws and regulations[3]—a leviathan undertaking, which pried open a great many markets for Western firms.

But in a way that's markedly different from Japan in the 1970s and '80s, China has undergone a sudden, deep—and unprecedented—integration with the U.S. and Asian economies. The volume of trade between China and its neighbors has shot through the roof. From 1993 to 2003, two-way trade between China and Japan grew over 250 percent; with Taiwan, over 300 percent; with Korea, 670 percent; with

Malaysia, 1025 percent; with Singapore, 350 percent; with the Philippines, 1800 percent; with Thailand, 835 percent; and with India, 1025 percent. Consequently, its regional trading partners are running massive trade surpluses with China.

An important dynamic to understand is that the total Asia Pacific trade deficit with the United States has not risen in the last fifteen years—and that includes China's contribution. As China imports energy, raw materials, and components from its neighbors to make the products it exports to the world, the overall trade deficit has simply shifted from Japan, South Korea, Taiwan, and Hong Kong to China. In other words, Asia is still selling as much to the United States as it always has—the goods are just flowing through the mainland first, vaulting China from the thirtieth-ranked trading nation in the world in 1977 to number three in 2006.[4]

You can open your markets as wide as you want, but if your economy's a dog, no one's going to do business with you. China's developing economy is so popular because it dovetails with its more advanced trading partners. China excels at lower value, commodity manufacturing, and assembly; we excel at advanced and applied technologies and services. This congruence has fueled the gargantuan volume of trade between the United States and China. And it's fused the economies together in a tight embrace.

Ever wonder why China's factories hum day and night? Why China scours the globe for raw materials, driving up the price of steel, plastic, and other inputs? Why China's demand for energy keeps surging, driving up the price of oil? It's mostly to keep pace with the U.S. demand for Chinese goods. U.S. demand powers Chinese demand. U.S. demand is sucking China into modernity.

As the two economies fuse together, there are very few areas where the United States and China directly compete, at this time. Surging imports from China generally do not displace U.S. industries and eliminate jobs. Most of the goods America imports from China (clothes,

toys, housewares, and the like) are low-value products whose manufacturing left the West decades ago—for Japan, Hong Kong, Taiwan,
and South Korea in the 1970s and '80s, and later for Latin America and
Southeast Asia in the 1990s.[5]

Yet as American demand for Chinese goods keeps rising, everyone
is waiting for the tide to flow the other way. Everyone is waiting for
Chinese demand for American goods and services to pick up—
especially as U.S. household savings sink deep into the red for the first
time since the Great Depression, and the U.S. government has been using the Chinese central bank as its corporate credit card.

Enter China's middle class—a pool of new consumers that already
outnumbers the combined populations of the United Kingdom and
France.[6] As these modern, urban consumers enter the market, they
want all the premium goods and services that their money can buy
(and which China cannot provide)—from finished goods and applied
technologies to food and pharmaceuticals, from financial and consulting services to advertising and architecture.

As China's leviathan middle class emerges, China is becoming a major importer. Demand for imported goods and services will drive
China's ongoing integration with the world's economies; and that is
where the real business opportunity lies.

As China's pie gets bigger, the pie gets bigger for all of us. China's
gains are our gains.

FLAT WRONG

By the time we reach the bus depot, it has gotten quite late. We
glimpse the drivers through an open door, huddled around a smoky
table. They are hard old men, with black nubs for bridgework, and
they are shouting at each other. Minnie Pearl strides into the room and
asks whether anyone can take us to Ningbo. They eye him warily.
They're all going to Hanzhou, a city that is on the way to Ningbo.
They will take us to Ningbo for a price.

My partner barks, cajoles, lectures, leaves—walking out into the parking lot three times, and each time is chased back into the depot. An hour later at 1:00 a.m, with tickets in hand, we have saved the equivalent of three dollars and eleven cents.

The bus has beds instead of chairs—double-decker bunk beds, lined up end-to-end along the dark cabin. That's a new one for me. I had seen some crowded Greyhounds, but never a mobile dormitory.

I trip on a body. People are lying prone in the aisle. I see the outline of shoulders. I guess these folks opted for the cheaper fare. It gives a new meaning to "standing room only." I knee my way onto the upper berth and suddenly wonder how many of these top-heavy death traps topple over in accidents.

That won't be a problem on this trip. Late-night construction along the highway chokes the traffic, and we inch our way to Ningbo. It takes over seven hours to get there. I stare out into the night. Is it really that dark outside, or is that just dirt on the window? I see a long band of dainty pink lights twinkling in black grime.

I'm wondering why we're going to Ningbo at all. Shanghai, so I've been briefed, excels at high-tech manufacturing, but Ningbo apparently excels at light industry: mechanical and electromechanical applications, plastic injection molding, tooling, and the like. The thinking is that Ningbo might present more fertile ground for a start-up. You can't just walk into a Shanghai semiconductor plant and start to do business with them. I see the logic, though I wish we had set out in Shanghai, if only to have avoided this unnerving, horizontal bus ride into the night.

Sometime later, we get to the hotel. I learn that there's a big difference between "tourist class" hotels, which cater to Western travelers, and "domestic" hotels, which cater to Chinese. We opt for a domestic hotel to save a yuan or two. It proves illuminating.

That night, I peer through the fumes of jet lag at *The Jeffersons* dubbed in Chinese. George sounds like a four-hundred-pound sumo wrestler. His voice is deep and gruff. "Weezy" is about all I can make

out. It seems culture is an export, too. The Chinese are building Confucian institutes of learning throughout Asia, Africa, and Latin America. We're exporting Norman Lear and Bud Yorkin.

Rice congee and tea for breakfast, and we're on the road. I'm actually feeling rested. For some reason, adjusting to the twelve-hour time
difference is easier for me than adjusting to the six hours' difference
with Europe. My brain doesn't feel like cool, damp cotton. China, here
we come!

First stop: Ningbo's famous Plastics City. We're going to canvass
our potential customer base. We think there might be an opportunity
for us to service China's $18 billion plastic resin market. We believe
that the Internet can help improve the distribution of plastic resins
into Ningbo's fragmented base of plastic injection molders, perhaps
through an online collective buying hub. We head out to Plastics City
to test our thinking.

It's about an hour's drive outside of Ningbo. We take a cab from the
hotel. Most taxis in China today are made by the successful Volkswagen joint venture, a testament to what a Western company can do in
China if they play smart and are persistent. Santana, the most common brand of taxi, is not Volkswagen's greatest triumph, though. In
engineering, it's one step above a rickshaw and lacks the ventilation.
The roads out of town are rutted with deep potholes and ditches, and
the car lurches and rattles.

I'm wearing a suit for some ridiculous reason, and the Chinese summer broil pierces my antiperspirant. I'm leaking through my garments. A tape of Britney Spears plays on continuous loop. We hear
Side A and Side B in succession, over and over again, as the hot chalky
dust starts to tickle my throat. I stare at the back of the driver's neck.
He's sweating too.

"Oops, I did it again . . . ," Britney clucks. I'm wearily nodding in
agreement.

We sputter into Plastics City. It looks nothing like what I had imagined. It's a grim old industrial park. Dingy factories are lined up in rows like vegetables in a garden. Here's a row that makes cigarette lighters. There's a row that makes motorcycle parts.

Most newcomers are shocked when visiting their first Chinese factory. The methods and modes of production appear slapdash, primitive, and sometimes unsafe. The jobs you see workers doing are usually a kludge system the plant manager has whipped together to fill orders and keep the factory going. They lack technology, they lack know-how, and they lack the capital needed to invest in better equipment—so they improvise.

This is the Chinese manufacturing juggernaut everybody is so afraid of?

Our driver finds the plant we're meant to visit first, an air conditioner manufacturer, and we're ushered through the gates. Here comes the general manager, a man in his fifties with a slack face. He is wearing a golf shirt and khakis. Golf has become somewhat of a craze in China, especially among businesspeople. China's dearth of arable land lends a certain debauched cachet to the pursuit of golf. You'll often see business managers in golf shirts these days.

His flat stare gives him away. He looks like a trauma victim. He's a member of the "lost generation," as children of the Cultural Revolution are dubbed. They are usually fodder for the ranks of the last state-owned firms and are often considered untrainable by Western companies. The totality of their schooling and professional experience has taught them that "group thinking" is better than "individualistic thinking." They tend, therefore, to lack initiative, imagination, and accountability.

We tour the factory, then file into a conference room. We try to figure out where this prospective customer's needs lie, how we can help him become a more efficient operator. We ask questions about his suppliers and his buyers. How he buys, how much, from whom, and how often. We talk to him about the Internet.

Sure, he's got the Internet hooked up to his computer. That confirms our research: that Internet penetration among factories is high. But his secretary prints out the pages for him to read. He doesn't actually work the keyboard himself. Using the Internet for more than e-mail is a foreign concept to him. The notion of applications, of networked services, is nonexistent.

In the United States, the Internet acts as the central nervous system connecting the various companies that must collaborate to bring a product or service to market. It allows them to manage information, money, time, and resources—plus deal with any disruptions—in real time. Today, project managers are able to track each step of their cycle with precision and transparency (something supply-chainers call "visibility").

In China, however, paper is still the primary medium of commerce, so business is slow, expensive, nontransparent, and rife with human error. Unlike India, whose growth industries often employ the Internet as a distribution channel to deliver outsourced software and services, China's bricks-and-mortar manufacturing base has had little use for the Internet.

We visit factory after factory, and the situation is the same. It would seem that all the statistics are missing an important point: yes, Internet "penetration" is high, but Internet aptitude is still very low. Lots of Chinese businesses are hooked up to the Internet. They just haven't a clue how to use it.

And then it suddenly hits me. The world is still round. The Internet is just one example. Its adoption may be spreading to faraway countries like China and India, but huge disparities still exist in how it's applied. Putting the whiteboard models and the theories of globalization aside, this crucial difference can cost you big money when you're doing business.

To be sure, the world *is* flattening in many ways. The celebrated evolutionary biologist Stephen Jay Gould posited that the evolution of species sometimes throttles forward in sudden leaps. The flat world concept applies this thinking to economics: that innovations in technology sometimes drive radical, rapid transformation in societies. Indeed, it would appear that information technologies are spurring such change today, knitting together and transforming communities around the world.

And if you combine the proliferation of information technologies with other flattening forces—such as innovations in global logistics that allow us to transport more goods to more places than ever before; the emergence of English as the international language of commerce, letting us do businesses nearly everywhere; and the conjoining of the world's nations in multilateral groups like the WTO that bind them to common rules, regulations, and standards—then it's evident how boundaries that used to exist among nations and peoples, impeding the flow of capital, goods, and ideas, are eroding.

But metaphors, however keen, get you only so far. In reality, the flat worldview obscures other dynamics that are important to understand—especially if you intend to do business overseas. Seeing the world as flat will distort your perspective of both the forest and its trees, both the big picture and the details. When you're doing business in-country, that will cost you time, money, and resources.

Consider the big picture first, the trends that help us construe the markets: jobs, trade, and globalization. Let's start with jobs. If you see the world as flat, it's easy to imagine we're competing with China "on a level playing field," that our highly paid workers are competing head-to-head with low-wage Chinese workers. We can see our jobs flowing to China like water seeking its own level. The flat world tilts east, and our jobs roll away to China like the tide.

How else can we explain the last gruesome decade? The United States fired over 11 percent of its manufacturing workers (more than two million Americans!) in just seven years from 1995 to 2002. The United Kingdom fired 12 percent of its workers in the same period;

Germany, 6 percent, Sweden, 7 percent, and Japan, a staggering 16 percent.[7]

In the news media, these numbers are usually reported alongside China's overall gains in gross domestic product (GDP): "The United States lost another 425,000 manufacturing jobs this month, while China continues to surge ahead at 9.8 percent growth." The implication: that our jobs are headed overseas and are fueling China's expansion.

Guess again. China fired over 15 percent of its workers from 1995 to 2002, beating most of the world in job losses.[8] Where are the jobs going, if not to China? Factory employment has been sinking around the world for a decade—not just in the West—as part of a global employment recession. Firms everywhere have been firing workers and investing in technology to stay competitive. This grim strategy seems to be paying off. Global industrial output rose more than 30 percent between 1995 and 2002, reflecting gains in efficiency despite the deep cuts in labor.

Job losses in the West, then, do not necessarily add up to China's gain. The popular notion that for every American manufacturing job there's a cheaper labor source in China is simply untrue. In fact, jobs in the West often have no equivalent in China.

Consider the plastic sacks that the local supermarket uses to bag your groceries. Making these bags became an automated process in the West decades ago, but China still often makes them by hand. Instead of using modern filming machines, Chinese workers knead and stretch the plastic like bakers.

The Chinese bag factory will eventually buy modern filming machines, and the kneaders and rollers will all be out of work. A great many jobs, in fact—from factory workers to functionaries up and down the supply chain—will soon be obsolete in China.

Contrary to popular opinion, then, it's not a level playing field at all. American industries and labor are light-years ahead of Chinese industries and labor—in both the manufacturing and service sectors. In manufacturing, the skill of our workforce, the sophistication of our equipment, process, and corporate culture, dwarfs China's capability. In many cases, China is fifty years behind in technology and know-how. What's more, China is just starting to comprehend the importance of services—at the precise moment when China's growing manufacturing sector and middle class *need these services*. So in addition to manufacturing, American service industries have a huge head start and a tremendous edge over Chinese companies.

It's going to take time for China to evolve. The Chinese need to train a whole new generation of workers and management, as well as upgrade their capability by several orders of magnitude. That's time for the American workforce to prepare—and for American industry to build Chinese market share.

In addition to jobs, the flat worldview also distorts our picture of trade. Take a trend like surging imports from China. If you see the world as flat, you'll tend to view this as an assault on our economy. The flat world tilts west again—and a tidal wave of cheap merch rolls out from China, smacks against our shores, and leaves the wreckage of American businesses and jobs in its wake.

But trade between China and the West is often circular, not linear. Because of the complementary nature of our economies, surging Chinese imports in one sector usually trigger surging U.S. *exports* in another—a "virtuous circle"—creating profits, value, and jobs.

Let's take the apparel industry as an example of how this dynamic works. After a worldwide quota system on textiles, the Multi-Fiber Agreement, expired on January 1, 2005, U.S. imports of apparel from China shot through the roof, and in 2005 they were running at an average of 54 percent ahead of 2004.[9] But some imports accelerated even faster. Imports of Chinese cotton trousers and knit shirts rose more than 1,000 percent over 2004's imports, according to the U.S. Office of Textiles and Apparel.

The West is up in arms. Congress has been calling for trade restrictions and tariffs, and the EU has launched a formal investigation.

One small overlooked fact, though, is that China must import cotton to make all these garments. Who is the largest cotton exporter to the world? The United States. So the surge in U.S. apparel imports from China has been a windfall to U.S. cotton farmers. Cotton exports to China rose 300 percent in 2004 in anticipation of 2005 production after the quota's expiration. You can see this dynamic play out in many other industries, like steel, pulp, and plastics.

Determining where you fit on the virtuous circle of trade will help you position your business for future growth. If you are in manufacturing, dissect your product into its component parts. Plot where the inputs are coming from—all the way along the supply chain to the original raw material supplier. In many cases, your product or one of its components will fit somewhere along a virtuous circle of trade.

Many services also occupy a place on the virtuous circle. As Chinese enterprises and consumers modernize, they import more and more services from Asia and the West. And as Chinese firms enter the U.S. market, they overwhelmingly require the help of U.S. consulting, accounting, legal, and insurance firms to survive.

Labor can benefit from the virtuous circles of trade, as well. Not all unions are frothing at the mouth today. The longshoremen understood China's importance long ago and have fought hard for a place in the virtuous circle of global trade. As a result, longshoremen are far and away the highest-paid blue-collar workers in the United States today. Average salaries top $120,000 a year, based on 2,000 hours of work. Compare that to the average salary of a worker at one of the Big Three auto plants: $74,500 per year based on 2,000 hours of work, according to the Center for Automotive Research.

When the first shipping containers arrived in the Port of Newark in 1958, the longshoremen saw innovation as either a dire threat or a golden opportunity. They fought hard against the adoption of the container because it made a job that normally took twenty-one men take six. But before conceding, the union was able to wring a crucial concession from the ports as compensation: the container royalty fee, a three-dollar vig the union gets paid for every container cleared.[10]

Judging by container traffic today—the U.S. West Coast handled more than 20 million containers in 2005, and the number is rising—that was a clairvoyant bit of commercial extortion. But perhaps even more wisely, the longshoremen started negotiating partnerships with international brethren and affiliated unions, like the truckers' union. They were thinking in terms of global markets (and therefore global unions) before people were even thinking in terms of national markets and national unions. They understood that the benefits of trade are circular, and that if they positioned themselves at a node in the flow of goods, they would maintain their relevance and power.

Though the sea containers made traditional stevedoring obsolete, the union adapted: it trained its members to operate the cranes that move the containers from the ships to the terminals. If you've ever visited a modern port, you'll notice immediately the lack of people on the docks. Giant cranes move the containers around like Lego blocks. High in the air, the longshoremen sit in glass-enclosed cabs and manipulate the big machines. On windy days, they say, the cabs lurch back and forth.

The union used strong tactics to make sure its members were the ones moving the cargo, no matter the mode. The West Coast port strikes in 2002 again demonstrated their canny ability to adapt, turning adversity into opportunity. The longshoremen were locked out of twenty-nine major ports on the West Coast for ten days at an estimated cost of $1 billion a day to the U.S. economy.[11] Ships circled out at sea, while factories began to sputter to a halt. Auto plants, for instance, went dark after four days, as their lean inventories of component parts ran dry. The lockout left the longshoremen in a stronger position. While the ports won the right to implement new software that uses global positioning to track cargo, the union won the right for its members to operate that software.

The longshoremen are a good example of a union that understands that the world is not flat, that the benefits of trade flow in a virtuous circle; and despite technological advancements that threaten to make the union's members effectively obsolete, it's been able to maintain its position in the global supply chain through adaptation and grit.*

Like the longshoremen, if you see the world as round, you'll see that what goes around, comes around: China's gains are often our gains, too. But the flat worldview precludes this point of view.

The flat worldview also misconstrues China's might in the global economy. Spied across the plane of a flat world, China seems like a menacing Mack truck bearing down on us. It looks like we're about to be rammed at full speed.

China's economy is still a pipsqueak, though. It's a fraction of the U.S. economy. In 2005, our GDP was about $12.5 trillion. China's was about $2.25 trillion.[12] As a frame of reference, Japan, the largest national economy after the United States, achieved a GDP of about $4.5 trillion in 2005. Only the Euro Zone—a collection of countries—rivals the U.S. GDP in size.

Even with China's breakneck pace of growth, then, its GDP is not expected to reach Japan's 2005 level until the year 2020. China is more akin to the Little Engine That Could than to a menacing Mack truck. China chug-chugs along—"I *think* I can, I *think* I can"—overcoming ramshackle infrastructure, primitive technologies, crippling poverty, and rampant corruption through its sheer force of will and an infusion of capital from the West.

Yet China looks large in our rearview mirror partly because of the metrics we use to describe it. We bake the notion of parity—of

*For more case studies, visit AllTheT.com/cases.

flatness—into the very data. For example, when economists talk about purchasing power parity (PPP), they make a set of assumptions about how far the yuan will go in buying goods and services for the Chinese in comparison to the dollar. Using PPP metrics, then, people earning $14,000 a year in China are considered "middle class" because they can afford to buy the amenities of a middle-class existence—when in the United States, that person would be considered below the poverty line. Indeed, China is the world's first "poor superpower," but in a flat world, we miss the "poor" part of the picture.

The flat worldview will distort your picture not only of the forest but also of the trees. When you're doing business in China, you're going to get your head handed to you if you place your faith in the much-ballyhooed "flattening forces" of technology, economic integration, and multilateral organizations.

Yes, the Internet allows us to link up directly with Chinese factories, but it transports the chaos of China's in-country supply chain right into your Sheboygan office. Yes, our two economies are integrating, but the mainland is a thicket of local dialects, laws, and customs. Yes, China has adopted international business standards and practices, but it's far from compliant. (Do you use GAAP? Sure, I wear their khakis.)

When it comes to commerce, the basic problem with the flat worldview is that it posits parity as an organizing principle. I've seen business guides, for example, that suggest if your product sells well locally in the United States, it'll probably sell well abroad. In other words, what plays in Peoria will play in the provinces. This couldn't be further from the truth.

THINK DIFFERENT

To succeed in China, you'll need to see how things are different, not the same. It's easy for newcomers to get taken in by the similarities between our two systems. We see a reflection of ourselves in China's embrace of entrepreneurialism and the profit motive. But the illusion of sameness occludes critical differences between China and the West—differences that will cost you time and money.

In an illustration of this phenomenon, the renderings of the cat and pig below appear the same except for a single squiggle on the pig's tail.

In China, habit and instinct compel Westerners to focus on the similar bodies and ears of the cat and the pig, only to miss the squiggle—the illuminating difference. I would learn that lesson the hard way, the first time we shipped goods from Long Beach, California, to Shanghai on regular wood pallets, the kind so ubiquitous in transportation—only to discover China's fear of foreign wood blights, and its special requirements for wood fumigation documents before clearing customs. We had not submitted the required documents, so the goods were seized and held for a week as we wrangled with Chinese port authorities to get them released.

In this case, habit made us overlook the squiggle, the illuminating difference: unlike the United States, China has very few forests. So an imported wood blight, from something even so innocent as pallets, could devastate the little forestation the country has. Suddenly, the irrational fear seemed more reasonable.

If you tug on that squiggle a little more, other illuminating differences appear. China's few forests mean that cardboard is scarce. What little cardboard there is gets recycled over and over again. So the cardboard boxes that China uses to export goods are usually inferior—

Cat   **Pig**

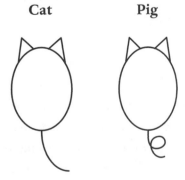

second- and sometimes even third-rate. Ryder Systems, the truck renter turned global logistics provider, learned that lesson the hard way when a thirty-foot wall of televisions they were warehousing for Philips collapsed. The inferior Chinese boxes on the bottom caved in.

Seeing the illuminating difference helps prevent costly mishaps like these. It also helps you detect new markets for your products. If China has few forests, then wouldn't the pulp to make paper be scarce? Yes, pulp *is* scarce in China, and pulp has quickly risen to become a major Chinese import from the United States—it's often sent to China for processing into paper before getting reexported back to the West.

Here's another one: China has no aftermarket in plastics. Its consumers don't recycle, and its factories use most of their scrap. So China manufacturers hungrily seek recycled and reground resins on the world markets as a low-cost alternative to virgin materials. This represents a big and relatively untapped opportunity for the recycling industry in the United States, which is dominated by small and mid-sized firms.

Discerning difference not only will help you identify new markets, it will improve your odds for success. My partner and I, however, see only sameness. We presume the Internet to be a great flattener in China, and we are flattened instead.

We meet with hundreds of Chinese factories in hopes of linking together an online buyers' consortium for plastic resins. But try as we might, we cannot build demand for our services. Because their plants are chugging day and night, because they are actually turning away new orders, these factory owners cannot see the value in buying plastics more efficiently, much less over the Internet. In a flat world, our model would have worked. In the real (round) world, it tanks.

We do give it our all, though. A real Madison Avenue rollout. We carpet-bomb Ningbo with publicity. Some strings are pulled, and I'm suddenly sitting in a high-backed chair alongside Ningbo's powerful mayor. Flanking us are the heads of various ministries. ("Sit up straight!" one of my staff whispers to me.) Tea is served as we discuss technology and communications infrastructure and the plastics market in Ningbo. The next day, I keynote a United Nations conference on trade and e-commerce. We're trying to build some visibility of our corporate brand, and putting the round-eye in front is a calculated ploy. Let the callow kid from the Sunshine State play the beard.

Meanwhile, we've got an uptown logo, fancy cards, some nice-looking baseball caps, a snazzy Web site, and zero business. We're burning through our equity capital, too. Big staff in Ningbo, big staff in New York. Time to punt. If one hypothesis tanks, try another.

3

ORIENTING YOURSELF

Deng's Law of Uncertainty: "One never knows, do one?"

We're in scramble mode. What assets can we leverage? Well, we've got a Web site address that's potentially saleable. (Having "China" in our URL boosts its street value.) But that's a one-off.

More significantly, we have a database—a list of hundreds of factories and regional raw material suppliers, firms we'd met and inspected. Instead of selling to these companies, we could sell *for* them.

We're back on familiar territory, targeting U.S. firms as customers. Our China myopia dissipates, and we come to our senses a bit. We home in on the market. We know the competition is stiff: there are scores of China importers, agents, jobbers, and manufacturers' reps in the marketplace. We'll have to differentiate ourselves.

Our service proposition, we decide, will not begin with the notion of cheap Chinese products. It will begin, instead, with customer need: small and midsized U.S. companies scrambling to get into China and having a tough go of it. After meeting with many potential clients, we will come to understand that every company has unique needs in terms of product mix, timing, and inventories. Buyers, we will learn, are not so much looking for cheaper product lines per se. They're looking for a comprehensive China solution—engineering, manufacturing, quality control, logistics.

To give ourselves a fighting chance, we decide to avoid industries that are already saturated with Chinese imports, like apparel, housewares, and toys. We focus instead on goods that require some engineering and technical know-how to make, goods that must live up to tough U.S. standards—auto parts, building supplies, medical and dental supplies, heating and air conditioning parts, and the like. Companies in these industries will no doubt be struggling to import Chinese products that are reliably compliant with stringent U.S. regulations. And Chinese factories will, in turn, be struggling to upgrade their capability to meet U.S. demand. We can add value by helping both sides get what they want.

We invest in expanding and deepening our supplier network, so we can manufacture products made of metals, rubber, and paper, in addition to plastics. Our new business model is to act essentially as a channel integrator: to knit together suppliers in China that can deliver products tailored to our customers' needs. We will disintermediate the low-value players, saving money and time for our clients and commanding nice margins for ourselves. Or, at least that's what it says on the PowerPoint presentation.

The reality in China would prove very different from our expectations, of course.

ACTS OF GOD, FORCES MAJEURES, AND MONDAY MORNINGS

China is the land of the unexpected. Disaster just falls out of a clear blue sky. As you get acclimated to doing business on the mainland, you'll get better at forecasting. But sometimes you'll be blindsided by an event that could only be called an act of God or a force majeure.

A vicious typhoon will come ripping through the town, and your factory will suddenly shut down for days. Or a big, nasty dust storm will descend on the city, putting your timetable on indefinite hold. Or the power supplying your factory will suddenly sputter out, as the whole city goes dark for a week in a massive blackout.

While you can't prevent acts of God from striking, you can hedge against them. Rather than put the whole operation in peril, China business vets set up alternative suppliers outside of China, in case of emergency. Some choose local sources. Others also look to countries like Vietnam, Mexico, or Estonia. And even within China, they arrange for backup suppliers, in case something goes haywire with their factories under management.

This is a lesson I'd learn the hard way. I'd always seem to get whacked on Monday mornings. Everything would be going fine, when suddenly the ten plagues of Egypt would come raining down from the sky, and we'd miss our deadlines. Time and time again, I'd be caught without backup suppliers in place. Do as I say, not as I do.

THE ACCIDENT OF CHINESE CAPITALISM

Acts of God aside, China is a nation in such intense flux that the unexpected becomes the usual. Anything can happen—and does. In fact, Chinese capitalism itself was an accident.

When Deng took over Mao's Soviet-styled economy, he saw that most of China's unwieldy state-owned sector was uncompetitive in the global markets. These companies would be roadkill as soon as any serious foreign entrant was allowed into China. So Deng sought to revive the moribund state sector by spinning off nonperforming assets and relaxing the rules of business ownership to encourage competition and innovation.

But something unexpected happened, a consequence that not even the clairvoyant Deng foresaw. While his eyes were trained on the state-owned sector, "a strange army appeared from nowhere. . . . All sorts of small enterprises boomed in the countryside," he reflected in 1987.[1] Deng didn't imagine his reforms would prompt an eruption of new businesses. He'd unintentionally struck entrepreneurial oil.

Many presume China's "economic miracle" was concocted in some dark room, by a cabal of Commie planners. Often, when India's economic rise is compared with China's, the false dichotomy of India's "micro entrepreneurialism" versus China's "macro state planning" is cited.

Actually, small businesses (a sudden, gushing wellspring of them) were the innovators and transformers of China's economy. And they didn't figure at all in China's plan for modernizing.

Thousands of sudden new entrants to the marketplace drove the destruction of the old command system and supplanted it with a homegrown, hurly-burly marketplace. Up and down the Pearl River Delta, entrepreneurs rushed headlong into ventures with low capital requirements, like making shoes, apparel, and toys. Remarkably, as the dismantled state-owned sector was shedding jobs, new entrants to the marketplace were absorbing them.

Many agrarian societies (whether Communist dictatorships or otherwise) have sought to transform their economies into modern marketplaces. They have privatized state-owned assets. They have even enacted laws and regulations favorable to starting up, running, and unwinding businesses. But the missing—and critical—ingredient in most cases has been the ferment of entrepreneurialism.

New businesses innovate and compete to survive. They create jobs and train the workforce. State-owned assets that have been privatized, on the other hand, tend to underperform. They're saddled with legacy systems, employees, and business culture.

Deng merely relaxed the rules of business ownership, allowing entrepreneurs to partner with their local municipality. But that was more than enough. In a country with no contract enforcement, no banks to support you, no protection from government shakedowns, going into business with your town gave you a lot of cover. If you needed start-up capital, your village government would help. If you needed a contract enforced, your town leadership would back you up. If you needed protection from a shakedown, the municipality would provide it.

This new class of business ownership, the town and village enterprise (TVE), took off like gangbusters. Share of China's industrial output by TVEs rose from 9 percent in 1978 to 30 percent in 1991. And virtually none of the increase in China's output came from spun-off state-owned assets—practically all of it is attributable to these newly formed firms.[2] By the mid-1990s, most of the TVEs would, in turn, be privatized, the municipal governments' equity sold to individual owners.

Today, the private sector produces over 40 percent of China's GDP—and that number is rising fast.[3] If the birth of Chinese capitalism, the bellwether of the economy, was accidental, imagine the unexpected events you'll encounter just going about your day-to-day business.

TECHNIQUES TO KEEP UNCERTAINTY AT BAY

Our first real lead comes from the milk industry. We're tasked with sourcing a plastic molded part that goes into a milk-processing machine. This should have been an easy win, but we underestimate the role that uncertainty plays in even the most routine jobs in China, and how it can cost you everything.

We get a sample of the product from the customer and must dispatch it to our China office, so that the job can be bid out to a group of factories. My partner and I are standing there with a plastic thingamabob in our hands, puzzling over how best to get it to Ningbo. *(How many Ivy Leaguers does it take to screw in a lightbulb?)*

We decide to send it via FedEx. On the form, it asks us to value how much the product is worth. We look at each other. Well, this is our first piece of business, and we do not want to muck it up. So it's worth a lot. We put $5,000 on the form. The actual value of the product is about a dollar thirty.

Dumb mistake. When the goods arrive in the port of Ningbo, they will not be released from customs until we pay several hundred dollars in duties, based on the value of the goods that we declared on the form and what product type it was.

It will be the first of many expensive flubs.

We clear the goods. (It is hard money to spend.) Then we set about locating a factory to handle the job. China does not make everything; nor does it make everything well. As it turns out, we know many factories that can handle making such a part. But we do not have a firm grasp on whether the factories under management can make a part that lives up to FDA regulations.

Any product distributed in the United States that comes in contact with food or drink—whether it's a component in food-handling equipment or a storage container like Tupperware or even a faucet—must comply with tough standards. The regs mostly seek to prevent the leaching of raw materials into the food. Stringent requirements govern the raw material content as well as the construction and performance of the product. Different standards bodies sometimes regulate the same product.

We assume that a reg is a reg—it's a certainty—and that the factory will understand this. They don't. America, EU, and Japan have the highest standards in the world for product quality and integrity, and we assume that Chinese factories involved in export understand the basic notion of complying with a reg. This is not always the case.

Sniffing an opportunity for big profits, we choose to work with the cheapest-quoting factory in the group, and then realize after a few weeks down the road that complying with the regs is going to be a problem. The factory keeps trying to skirt the rules. A reg is not necessarily a reg—not when it impinges on the gross profit margin.

By the time we locate a new factory that proves they understand how to comply with regulations, we will have lost some money, much time, and the customer. Here would have been an opportune moment to understand that in Mandarin, "cheap" and "inexpensive" mean the same thing.

MANAGING UNCERTAINTY
THROUGH APPREHENDING DIFFERENCE

Luckily you don't need to speak Chinese to succeed in China. But what we often assume as a certainty in the West is often not at all a certainty in China. If you can bear this in mind, many events that at first might seem unexpected to you will suddenly seem plausible— even predictable—once you understand the context.

In particular, be aware of some important idiosyncrasies in language, perception, and convention. To succeed in China, you'll need to see how these elements are different from how we operate, not the same.

Miscommunication can hobble every written and spoken engagement you undertake. It can leach time, money, and, eventually, the will to go on. How much time and money (and will) depends on you.

It's not just because the parsing of simple language becomes maddeningly hard. It's because the meanings *behind* the words are elusive. You and your counterparts might be using the same word—but with contrasting perceptions of its meaning. Imagine if that word is the very product you are trying to manufacture. Or a critical deal point. Simple mistakes can cost you everything.

Logic and Rhetoric

One key difference lies in the logic and rhetoric that govern business discourse. When it's time to talk business, China does exactly the opposite from the West. Europe and the United States prize brevity. Information is aligned in a top-down scheme. The main points are stressed first, and the supporting points are subordinated. The executive summary is followed by the plan, for example. The logic is deductive; the rhetoric, direct. In China, the logic and rhetoric work in reverse. Conventionally, information is built from the bottom up. Supporting details are provided first, and the main idea is subordinated. The logic is inductive; the rhetoric, indirect.

This can be infuriating to the uninitiated, as it would appear your interlocutors are trying to waste your time and confuse you. I remember a disastrous pitch for equity capital at a New York venture firm. I brought my partner along to kick off the meeting. Instead of opening with the main idea (why our firm would make a superior investment), he launches into a disquisition on the history of China's private sector since Chairman Mao, moves to the plight of the average Chinese worker, tells an anecdote about his brother, segues into a description of China's manufacturing base, and finally alights on why our firm would make a good investment.

Forty-five minutes later, we've come to rest on page one of our PowerPoint deck. Our audience is blankly staring into the middle distance. It's time to wrap up and go. My partner was merely being true to convention, of course—that it's often better to reach one's destination by means of a "zigzag bridge," as the old Chinese proverb goes. But to the bankers, we appeared disorganized and incompetent.

As if zigzagging weren't enough of a problem, Chinese translates clumsily into English. Simple concepts can seem nearly impossible to put across. A sign in my Ningbo hotel room once read, "Forbidden Heterosexual in the Room." What could this mean? Had I checked into the wrong sort of hotel?

Communication in China is often littered with these kinds of weird, unintelligible remarks, confounding Westerners and causing costly executional mistakes. A single missed word, for example, once sent my China agent serenely off to buy pumps from a lightbulb manufacturer. That was an expensive mistake.

But even if you understand what is being said, you may not understand what is being meant. Sometimes a concept in English simply doesn't have an analog in Chinese. This can be an especially ugly problem when the concept happens to be a tenet of Western corporation law, such as fiduciary duty, rights and obligations, or representations and warranties.

Take fiduciary duty as an example. Teachers who train Chinese managers in Western business say this concept is invariably one of the hardest to put across. A fiduciary, from the Latin *fiduciarius,* meaning "trust," is basically a trustee—one who is entrusted to act in good faith on behalf of another. In a typical American company, the officers and directors are fiduciaries. The owners entrust their capital to these executives, and they must, in turn, act in capital's best interests, under penalty of law. Capital is king. The officers and directors are its vassals.

The concept of fiduciary duty is the product of four hundred years of evolving jurisprudence in the West, since the first corporations were chartered by European governments in the seventeenth century. Chinese corporations, on the other hand, are a product of fifty years of evolution, since Mao set up a squad of state-run monopolies to fulfill his Five Year Plans.

Things have changed a lot since Mao. But today's typical Chinese corporation still relies on the federal or municipal government for funding. Capital is not a sacred trust. It's an entitlement. This is a key difference. If you plan to invest in a Chinese company, for instance, your capital will not be protected as it will in the West, nor will your Chinese partners feel any sense of being the sacred trustees of your money.

Fiduciary duty impacts everything from bookkeeping to boardroom business planning. In the United States, for example, corporations must keep consolidated books and publish accurate financial reports as part of their fiduciary duty to stockholders. In China, however, it is common to find several sets of books: a set for the investors, a set for management, a set for the suppliers, a set for the banks, and a set for the tax collector.

It's not a matter of fraud, but a matter of convention. Both China's newborn market system and its moribund planned system thrive on informality. If you're an entrepreneur in China, keeping your head low is the best way not to get it lopped off. That's partly why businesses often represent their numbers in such a way as to avoid excessive taxation and unwanted attention from the authorities. There's a disincentive to publish accurate numbers.

If you are working with a Chinese partner, therefore, you must always squint at the financial reports. First, make sure your Chinese team is on the same page with you in terms of basic definitions. How you define a sale may not correspond to how they define a sale, a basic difference that will throw all your numbers out of whack.

After definitions are clarified, you'll still need to verify every number with documentation. Insist that every single commercial document associated with a given order be reviewed by you: wire confirms, invoices, and bank statements are especially important. That way, you'll have a reliable basis of comparison, and you can vet your financial statements accurately.

In addition to financial reporting, the fact that there's no analog for fiduciary duty in China will also impact boardroom business planning. This fundamental misalignment can split a Chinese-American boardroom in two. One iteration of my board of directors was composed of three Americans and two Chinese. If you had asked the Americans to articulate their primary duty, they would have told you that it's to return as much capital to the owners as soon as possible. If you had asked the Chinese, you would have gotten a different story. One director would have told you that his duty was to foster the growth of private industry in China. The other would have told you his duty was to the greater glory of his family.

The Americans pushed hard for better margins and firmer cost controls. The Chinese pushed hard for sweetheart contracts for factory-owning friends and family back home. The board was cleaved into two competing camps, and one was working hard against the stockholders' best interests.

As China's leading corporations prosper and seek to penetrate markets in the West, they are investing in, and acquiring, companies in North America and Europe. How the newly thrown-together boards deal with the concept of fiduciary duty will have a lot to do with whether these companies succeed.

The bid from Chinese oil company CNOOC to acquire America's Unocal, for example, was doomed because of clumsy boardroom management. CNOOC, China National Offshore Oil Corporation, has focused much of its exploration and extraction in the South China Sea and is considered the most lean and modern of China's state-owned oil companies. Both Morgan Stanley and Goldman Sachs underwrote its public offering on the New York Stock Exchange (under the symbol "CEO"). Acquiring Unocal would have broadened CNOOC's Asian footprint (not U.S. footprint)—two-thirds of Unocal's assets are already in Asia.[4]

CNOOC was unaccustomed to having independent directors. It failed to apprise the outside directors of its plans to acquire Unocal (which could arguably be seen as a breach of their fiduciary duty to the stockholders). Had the company done so, and had it won approval of its plans, the outside directors would not have actively tried to scuttle the deal, which is what occurred.

But if the boardrooms and professional management trainers both struggle to put across the concept of fiduciary duty, you shouldn't waste too much time trying. Instead, do your best to understand the motives of your Chinese counterparts. This will help prepare you for how they will likely behave.

By and large, Chinese owners will want to make money for themselves and their family, ahead of their partners and investors. It's easy to understand why. It's a matter of survival. No effective social programs exist in China.[5] So if you contract a debilitating illness, you're bankrupt. A riot recently broke out in a Chinese town when a hospital refused to treat a young boy who drank pesticide, because the grandfather didn't have the cash on hand to pay for treatment. Making as much money as possible keeps your family alive. Bear this in mind, and simply take extra precautions.

For example, if you are sourcing goods from a Chinese supplier, try to predict where your counterparts might smell a chance to make a quick yuan. If there is a cheaper, lower-quality raw material that they can employ to make extra profit, be prepared for the likelihood that they will. There are many third-party quality assurance labs in China that you can hire to batch-check raw materials on your behalf before they get processed. (Just about every major third-party inspection company has offices in China—usually several.)

Or, if your China factory can cut corners by skimping on manufacturing control, work together to put quality and procedural documentation into place. Henry Schein, Inc., one of the world's largest distributors of medical and dental supplies, works with its China suppliers to build a binder before starting a sourcing program, which includes quality control, manufacture control, and procedural documentation. Schein and its partners then use that documentation as a basis for cooperation and discipline, as well as measuring and improving performance. Once you have a template, it can be replicated, with minor modifications, across suppliers.

Aside from taking these kinds of extra precautions, the best way to prevent fraud is to structure your deals in the true spirit of mutual profit and partnership. If you squeeze your suppliers to the point where they can't make money, they will surely screw you. If you allow them a decent margin, they will be less likely to do so. Aligning your commercial interest with your China partner is a time-tested way to increase your chances of success. Even Wal-Mart, whose buyers bludgeon Chinese suppliers within an inch of their lives, allows them to make enough margin to sustain operations.

Along with fiduciary duty, contractual rights and obligations have no analogy in China. Until recently, the very notion of a "right" didn't exist in Chinese legal history. For thousands of years, the emperor, and later the state, wielded absolute power. The populace were powerless, were entitled to nothing, and held no truths to be self-evident, save their subjugation to authority.

Thousands of years of Chinese jurisprudence, then, dealt solely with the punishment of crimes, meted out by fiat. There is an old saying in China, though: "Heaven is high, and the emperor is far away," meaning: "Do whatever you can get away with." Despite the best efforts of China's government to adopt a system ruled by laws, this lawless attitude is still commonplace in China business practice today.

A signed contract, therefore, is an invitation to start negotiating. Signatures mean nothing. Obligations are seen only as suggestions. Rights aren't comprehended at all. In many cases, the real negotiating will start *after* the contracts are executed. It is important, then, that when you negotiate terms with your Chinese partners, you review the concepts behind the words with great specificity, point by point.

Make sure they understand what they must *do* to live up to their end of the commercial and legal bargain that you strike. If your Chinese counterpart is responsible for trucking the goods to the port, go beyond the abstraction of who holds title to the goods. Your counterpart might nod his head and say he understands the concept of title, but make sure it's clear: If the truck breaks down on the way to the port and the goods are damaged, who is responsible? The factory? The trucking company? You? This must be spelled out clearly.

Issues like these are crucial to sort out first—so you can avoid litigation later. While China's courts are more hospitable to contract enforcement today than ever before, the threat of a lawsuit will not deter your Chinese partners from breaching an agreement. They will see themselves as having a home-court advantage when it comes to navigating the court system. Whether or not this is true, you should try to avoid the expensive and time-consuming hassle of litigation and employ other methods to enforce your contracts.

Think in terms of carrots and sticks. If you are investing capital into a joint venture, don't transfer all the money at once. Coordinate your payments to coincide with the completion of milestones on your partner's side. Be warned. Many Chinese businesses are undercapitalized and employ old technology. So a typical business owner will often do anything, or say anything, to secure capital and modern technology. Rights and obligations? Okay. Signed contracts? Sure. But once the transfer of capital and technology has been secured, anything goes.

If you are sourcing goods from China, backload the payment until after you receive the goods and they're approved by your inspection. If you are selling goods into China, don't release the product until you are paid. If you haven't done business with a party before, avoid collection problems by having the China buyer escrow funds or purchase a letter of credit.

Another tenet of Western corporation law, the concept of representations and warranties, has no analog in China either. In the West, the notion of transparency is universally understood, and full disclosure is taken very seriously before a contract is executed. If false representations and warranties are made, the contract can be unraveled. In China, the concept of transparency has not taken hold. So a typical Chinese business owner will make any representation or warranty he thinks you will want to hear. Before you seal the deal, make sure you investigate your partner's claims.

You can't just call up Dun & Bradstreet and get an accurate report, though. You need to do your own gumshoeing. Try getting in touch with other U.S. or European customers with whom your Chinese party has done business to ascertain credibility. You should also contact the party's bank. China's government-backed banks are eager to attract foreign investment and trade into their municipalities. They'll take your call.

In particular, watch out for "triangular debt," which pervades China's market economy. One party will owe money to another, who in turn will owe money to still another; and all three will collapse if one of them defaults. To investigate triangular debt, in addition to contacting the party's bank, you should contact their principal suppliers. If the party in question is a plastic injection molder, for instance, call up their main resin supplier. Find out if the factory pays for its raw materials on time. Find out how long the factory has been doing business with the supplier. Usually the supplier will be forthcoming with this kind of information, because you are perceived to have deep pockets and could be a source of new and repeat business for them.

Calling banks and suppliers is helpful, but there is no substitute for your own eyes. Go there. Look around. Tour the factories. Meet the owners. This will help substantiate their claims. If the factory is a dump, chances are they don't have the capital to improve it.

I once encountered a factory that claimed to be compliant with strict export standards—yet had no roof. I found this out the hard way. I imported a twenty-foot container of air vents for a leading U.S. home builder. The goods arrived soaking wet. It had rained on the roofless factory.

In deals that are complicated or involve a lot of capital, you should consider support from an international law firm. Firms with both U.S. and China practice areas can provide you with the benefit of a Western perspective combined with China executional ability. International firms will almost invariably cost you more money, but the fees will be well invested if your deal is big and more than just a trial order from a factory. No legal or commercial terms can be successfully negotiated, however, without trust.

BUILDING TRUST BEFORE PROFITS

Trust is a key element in any successful engagement in China. But you will not be trusted. The Chinese remember the last time they opened up to the West. They got the Opium Wars.

A widening trade imbalance started the conflict. Britain's thirst for tea was unquenchable in the early 1800s, and consumption per capita was doubling every year. Tea imports from India and China soared to keep up with consumer demand. But Britain's exports to China lagged. (Sound familiar?) To bring the trade imbalance into equilibrium, Britain started exporting opium to China, which was an illegal substance there. As usage spread, the Chinese authorities tried to impound all the dope they could lay their hands on.

To provide cover for their pushers, Britain attacked several Chinese coastal cities with its superior navy. China surrendered, and in 1842 a series of disastrous treaties were struck. China lost Hong Kong to Britain. China also had to open the vital ports of Shanghai, Ningbo, Fuzhou, and Guangzhou to British trade and residence.

The British kept exporting opium, and the Chinese kept trying to stop its spread. A second war started fourteen years later. The Chinese were defeated again. The British and French occupied the capital and torched the Summer Palace. China made still more painful concessions.

That was the last time China opened up to the West. And the Chinese remember the treachery and humiliation they encountered as if it happened last Tuesday. The wars are taught to schoolchildren and are the subject of many cautionary tales. It's no wonder that Chinese tend to distrust Westerners in business. "Screw unto them, before they screw unto us" is how they usually operate. In keeping with this sentiment, Westerners are called either "foreign devil," "round-eye," or "big nose," only partly in jest.

You can't erase history, but you can disabuse prejudice. Build trust and goodwill whenever you can. To this end, there is no replacement for face-to-face communication. While it's tempting to hide behind e-mail and phone, this is usually a big mistake. First, written communication tends to obfuscate. I often receive e-mails from China in which the words have been strung together as if at random, a Dadaist arrangement of commercial and engineering terms with no apparent syntactical meaning. Second, phone calls are difficult to coordinate because of the time difference, and picking through the words can take hours. Without meeting face-to-face, trust is difficult, if impossible, to establish.

But trust can be successfully built. And the more business you conclude with a Chinese partner, the more trust you will build. Be skeptical, though, if your counterparts implore you to put your sole trust in their personal connections—or *guanxi*—to get things done. In places where corruption and fraud are widespread, doing business with family or close friends makes sense. However, *guanxi* is no longer necessary to do business in China. Its importance has diminished considerably in recent years as the tendrils of law take root in China's civil society.

That's not to diminish the value of connections. Some businesses fall into a very gray area of enforcement and require support from the government or banks. Restaurants and bars are a good example. Making good with the local authorities and police in this case is just as critical as having all your papers in order. But if you don't have connections, don't worry. Good law firms can knit together these relationships for you.

Trust is necessary but not sufficient to succeed in China, though. Even the best-intentioned partners can work at cross-purposes. A thick fog of language and convention hangs between you, bending and refracting meanings like a prism. In order to get to the truth, or at least a mutually-agreed-upon truth, I have often employed a simple technique with great success.

THE 3 L'S: LISTENING, LOWER EXPECTATIONS, AND LEATHER ASS

Listening

Whether you are just getting started or are deep into a project, you need to listen strategically. As lawyers interrogate their witnesses, try to frame your dialogue by asking questions you already know the answers to, in order to build a foundation of knowns before proceeding to unknowns. You can't do your best Clarence Darrow imitation, however, until you get your bearings.

In any dialogue with China, the very first thing you need to do is get your ears comfortable with the accent you will be hearing. Start out with simple questions like, "When did you start your company?" or "Where is your factory?" or "What is the name of your plant manager?" Simple questions like these should elicit responses sufficient to get your bearings. Go slow. Listen as hard as you can.

Simple questions can also serve as a preliminary litmus test for the truth. That innocent question, "Where is your factory?" for example, once saved me from a catastrophe. A supplier I was considering doing business with had shut down its factory and moved in the middle of the night to avoid some run-in with a local bank. The hemming and hawing I got as an answer to my simple question set off alarm bells. I had uncovered a major stumbling block to trust, and severing talks saved me a lot of time, money, and heartache.

Once you've gotten acclimated, you can proceed into interrogation mode. Ask questions you already know the answers to in order to ascertain your interlocutor's particular brand of the truth. Of course, you will never know everything, but start with what you do know, before you move to what you don't.

I remember the time we contracted a Chinese supplier to make miniature flags for a leading wholesaler in the United States. The little flagpoles were made of a high-density plastic, which we were buying in virgin form because the client had strict product requirements like flexibility and durability. The factory struggled to produce a sample that met with the customer's approval, and scrap from rejected batches was building up. In frustration, the owner began secretly mixing the scrap into the new batches, regrinding the plastic and mixing it with the virgin, which saved him money but degraded product quality.

When we inspected the samples, they snapped like dry turkey wishbones. We went back to the supplier and employed the first of the three L's, listening strategically by framing the dialogue. We built "knowns" to elucidate the "unknowns." We walked through the whole manufacturing program together step by step. We asked, Who? What? Where? When? Why?

Starting from the beginning, we reviewed how the virgin materials got into the injection molding machines. The chief engineer had verified on the quality control documents that the materials were indeed the virgin resin. We knew this to be false. So we traced step by step who drove the forklift to the back of the stockroom to pick up the material, who inspected it, who fed it into the machines. We went slowly and asked a lot of questions. Our Chinese counterparts couldn't keep their stories straight. They hadn't expected such a grilling. The factory owner then started to retreat, admitting that he had switched the materials, but that he was entitled to do so. We had won a major concession.

We then moved on to the next issue: how the failure to produce a quality-compliant sample does not allow skimping on engineering. We kept hammering away until the owner finally agreed to bear the commercial costs associated with his misconduct (which up until now had been some minor DHL shipping costs—the real cost was lost time, which we unfortunately could not recover). The owner committed to work doubly hard to make a correct sample on the next iteration, which in fact he did, and the project went forward.

Lower Expectations

That meeting took seven hours. In China, you need to be prepared to spend a maddening amount of time covering very little ground, if advancing at all. You need to recalibrate your expectations of what you can achieve in a given allotment of time. A Western buyer's unrealistic timetables are frequently a cause of disrupted inventory. You expect the goods to be completed by a certain deadline. You find to your dismay that you have missed the mark by months.

For one thing, it's difficult just to align schedules. China is many time zones away. The time lag makes it hard to stay in synch, often having disastrous implications for project management. While this is typical of doing business with any Asian country, in China, it's important to minimize time lags whenever you can: other unforeseen factors that are mostly out of your control will extend your lead times too, like power shortages, and bureaucratic processing time.

So if you must call up your party in the middle of the night (or get awakened in the same way), then sleep be damned. If you forfeit a day here, a day there, very soon you've lost your profit margin, you've got disrupted inventory, and you're throwing good money after bad.

Of course, the ideal scenario is to be present *physically* where you are doing business. If your party is in Shanghai, then for key parts of the business cycle, you really ought to be in Shanghai. This will help build trust and understanding. It will also be much faster than slogging through phone calls and e-mails.

But don't expect the kinetic pace of New York (or even Hong Kong, whose stressed-out denizens go to New York to unwind). Though mainland China's coastal cities positively hum with commerce, things usually take a lot longer there. It takes a long time just to get around, for instance. Traffic in major cities like Beijing and Shanghai is always bad, but at rush hour, the highways turn into parking lots. Taxi drivers get out and start playing cards. This invariably occurs when you are late for an important meeting. I've sat for an hour in a single spot on the highway without moving, quietly having an aneurysm while my driver smokes, gambles, and has a grand old time with his pals.

Setting up meetings takes longer, too. You're not going to be able to nail three meetings in a day. Shoot for one. Processing papers takes longer, decisions take longer, everything takes longer.

But you're still saving a lot of time by being on location, because you're eliminating the delays inherent in e-mail and phone communication. And luckily, it's easier to get to China these days than ever before. A typical flight from New York to Shanghai used to take over twenty hours, tracing the globe's circumference by way of Los Angeles, then across the Pacific. Now planes fly over the Arctic and northern Canada, saving about ten hours in the air. A fourteen-hour flight still sounds long, but it's nothing compared to the marathon negotiating sessions you will encounter when you get there.

Leather Ass

You'll soon discover that to succeed you'll need a leather ass, a term of art used by champion poker players. It means having the guts and the perseverance to sit through a high-stakes match for as long as it takes to win, whether that's hours or even days. The strategies of leather-assed poker playing are exemplary for good negotiating and communication skills in China.

For example, your Chinese counterpart may intentionally slow the pace of negotiations. It's a common tactic to try to wear down the impatient Westerner who places a premium on time. If you're not willing to sit out negotiations, you're not going to achieve your objectives. Having a leather ass will show your Chinese partners that you mean business. It will also minimize further delays down the road. If you realize your counterpart is intentionally obfuscating to draw out negotiations, don't be afraid to cut through the bull. Repeat your direct, simple question again. Then again. And again. Keep doing it until you get a simple answer. Then verify that answer. Then move on to the next point. Try to keep framing and reframing the dialogue to get you closer to your meeting objectives.

After a full day sitting in a hot Chinese factory, your ass does tend to feel pretty leathery, too. You sip scalding green tea from little water cooler cups that melt into hot plastic jelly in your hands, and you wonder where your youth has gone. Hang in there. It is precisely in those moments that you need to remind yourself that by staying parked in that chair, you are actually *saving* yourself lots of time down the road.

I drink the tea not because I like the taste of molten polyethylene but because it shows respect. China's business customs differ markedly from those in the West. A gesture, for example, that causes your counterpart to lose face can be just as costly to you as a misunderstood word or concept.

FACE

The Chinese conception of "face" is widely misunderstood in the West. A commonplace expression in English, "to lose face" means to suffer embarrassment, and we assume this definition holds true in China. It doesn't. It misses the meaning—and its vital importance to the psyche. Face has a singular meaning to the Chinese, idiosyncratic to place, time, and culture, that evades direct translation.

The closest approximation to losing face in China is getting "dissed"—suffering disrespect or having one's dignity impugned. But it's not your reputation that is being dissed. It's your very being. As *thumos* and *gravitas* were central to the ancient Greek and Roman conceptions of self, so too is face to the modern Chinese. Face is self. To save face is to give the self its proper due. To lose face is to have the self dissed.

Many things will cause your China counterpart to lose face. Bad manners will, for instance. By the way Chinese will sometimes cut in front of you in line, masticate with gaping mouths, or disgorge gases and fluids in public, you'd think that manners do not play a significant role in Chinese mores. They do. Confucius wrote much of the primacy of manners, and manners are taught to Chinese children from the time they are infants. It's just that China's conception of manners is different from ours.

In restaurants, for instance, you will often see Chinese tap their index and middle fingers on the table when the waiter is pouring tea. It's a gesture that looks like the "Hit me" sign in blackjack. This tapping doesn't mean "Keep going" or "That's enough," though. It means "I bow to you." It alludes to a tale of how an emperor once changed places with his valet to move among his subjects anonymously. The disguised valet bowed to his master through this secret signal. Hardly the gesture of an impolite people. I have never seen a Westerner kowtow to a waiter.

You don't need to hold doors for your Chinese hosts or be the last out of the elevator. Don't worry about the attenuated niceties of Western manners. But you should treat your Chinese hosts with formality. Formality gives the face its due. Call the party "Mr." or "Ms." Dress formally (as much as the scorching heat or blistering cold will allow within reason).

Imagine that you are a foreign diplomat meeting the ambassador. You can wrangle all you want over terms, but you must pay respect to the office the ambassador holds. You can be as hard-nosed as you need to be. You can yell your head off, if you want to (they will). But never engage in ad hominem attacks. Never impugn their dignity. Formality and a sensitivity to face will usually be sufficient to dispel their assumption that you are an arrogant, treacherous foreigner and will help keep your negotiations on track.

Business Cards

In China, a business card is not a printed piece of paper. It's face. You can make your China counterpart lose face simply by the way you handle the card. You'll often encounter cards in China that run as long as résumés, the various board and executive positions printed on the front of the card, the back of the card, and even on fold-outs. This may seem odd and even comical to Westerners. Avoid your temptation to smirk at all costs. Your levity will be perceived as a grave insult.

The actual exchange is a piece of formal choreography I never tire of seeing. It's like a Japanese tea ceremony for cards. Watch your Chinese party's movements as they present their cards. You will need to imitate them both in receiving their cards and presenting your own.

1. Using both hands, grasp the card at the top two corners, gripping each corner between a thumb and forefinger, the letters of your name facing the receiver.
2. Extend the arms forward in a formal gesture of presentation.
3. Bow slightly at the waist.
4. Keep eye contact.

You are expected to receive the card in similar fashion, by bowing, extending your forearms, and grasping the card's two bottom corners with your thumbs and forefingers, as you maintain eye contact.

Give the card its due. Read it. The more you study the card, the more your party will feel as if they are being properly esteemed. Do not, under any circumstances, throw the card aside without reading it, or even worse, put the card in your wallet. That means you're sitting on the person's face. It shows tremendous disrespect. Westerners, who tend to present their cards at meetings as if casually dealing a hand of poker, often neglect this very important ritual and get the meeting off to a bad start.

Laughing and Breaking the Ice

Chinese do not consider laughing to be very dignified, especially in business settings. Laughing can undermine their confidence in your trustworthiness. The Chinese often employ the "deadpan" to great effect, maintaining a blank expression. You should strive to do the same. Don't break the ice with a joke or a personal anecdote. Though acceptable in the West, this will be seen as frivolous. The ritual of card exchanging is enough of an ice breaker. Then sit down to the table, fold both of your hands in front of you (an Asian posture that signifies you have nothing to hide), and get right down to business.

Drinking and Eating

Outside of the boardroom, however, all bets are off. The Chinese are famous for conducting business over raucous, boozy banquets. Though this behavior is less necessary than it used to be with the gradual decline of *guanxi,* many Chinese will still want to talk business with you over drinks and a meal. Except on rare occasions, do not feel as if you have to match your Chinese hosts in liquor consumption, shot for shot. Sampling is usually enough to show that you are open-minded and will be sufficient to save face. (If they press you, you can say your doctor has made you swear off alcohol.)

Of course, I learned that lesson the hard way. In one lunch meeting with a representative of the People's Congress, we each consumed an entire bottle of Wu Liang Ye, a clear Chinese grain liquor that is favored by hard-smoking, hard-drinking Chinese businessmen and politicians. It tastes vaguely like grappa but packs a punch like bathtub hooch. The Chinese consider this drink to be very strong. One shot would have sufficed to impress my host that I had the intestinal fortitude to do business with him. I wish I had known that in advance. By the end of the meal, twenty-four shots later, we had become bosom friends, but the viselike grip on my temples later that night will not soon be forgotten. Don't drink too much, and keep your wits about you.

The same basic principle applies to eating. Many of the dishes will appear exotic to the Western palate, even repulsive. Dog may be on the menu, for example. Don't gag or get on a soapbox. Your hosts will lose face. (You wouldn't like it either if a Hindu raked you over the coals for eating that gorgeous dry-aged porterhouse.)

Dog, as a matter of fact, is considered a great delicacy. There's a famous story of the vegetarian monks of the Xiaolin Temple. Dog was being roasted on the other side of a forty-foot wall, and they all used their superhuman kung fu strength to leap over the wall and eat the dog. It's said to be that good. (Though I can't say I've tried. I'm allergic to schnauzers.)

In general, Chinese do not consider eating a hazing ritual. So you don't have to eat the dog, and you don't have to eat the shrimp that are alive and writhing in a bowl of wine. But you do have to smile as your hosts bite the crunchy heads off and suck out the entrails. You're not allowed to flinch, shout out, or hide under the table.

If you want to signal that you're not interested in sampling, simply push the lazy Susan around, which passes the dish over to your neighbor. You can then cast your eye on the next dish, which you might just really enjoy. China's ancient cuisine is to Asia what French cooking is to Europe: it's considered the culinary fountainhead. I have sampled many wonderful dishes in China, dishes that cannot be savored anywhere in the United States.

Names

Traditionally, in writing or speech, names are inverted in China. Last name is followed by given name. It's important to establish up front which name is which, and then call them only by their last name or the last name–first name pair. If your party's first name is Yi and last name is Liu, for example, you would call him either just Liu or Mr. Liu or Liu Yi (with a stress placed on the "Yi"). Don't call him Yi. Chinese sometimes take English first names. They often adopt a close English approximation to their Chinese name: Dawei becomes David. Or they will adopt a name they've come across in a book or television show.

Hence, you tend to see some pretty colorful combinations—"Johnson Zhao," "Wellington Wang." I tend to shy away from the English names and stick to the respectful last name–first name formula. It is a small, but thoughtful, way to save face.

A lot of what you will encounter in China is different from what you'd expect—the logic and rhetoric, the concept of acceptable business practice, the notion of face. Blundering in any of these areas will cost you money and time. But trust is possible, and business success achievable. To be an effective communicator in China, you need only be open to—and capitalize on—the differences you will encounter there. Fortunately, the more business you do, the better you will get at this tricky anthropological exercise.

It's worth it. It'll not only tend to make you wealthier, it'll make you wiser. It will broaden your worldview. Often, you'll be the first Westerner a Chinese native has ever seen. You'll be ogled and pointed at as you walk down the street. Then you realize that meaning can masquerade in many forms. *You* know you are not a treacherous foreigner. But your bad reputation precedes you.

4

BUYING FROM CHINA

There are four of us—me, your big feet, and you.

It's autumn in New York, and the big blue sky mirrors the gorgeous income statement I'm reading. Topline growth that's doubling every year. And a gross profit margin so wide, you could drive a truck through it. While trading companies and other competitors are scraping by on 10 percent margins or less (the mugs), we're booking the kind of fat margins I remember from my days in the tech industry.

It's a mirage. The gorgeous day, the gorgeous financials, the gorgeous growth curve. It's another cold day in China, the hard, driving rain is the color of soot, and our orders are on the rocks. Our engineering team in Ningbo is telling us everything is hunky-dory, while the factories are failing to produce goods that are compliant with client specifications.

I'm wistfully humming bars of "Autumn in New York," while defective merchandise is quietly slipping by our quality control people. Defects are everywhere, on just about every order. The ringing phone wakes me from my reverie. Customers are withholding payment until requirements are met.

We stand behind our products. We eat the air shipping costs to expedite late orders, and we repair the defective merchandise. Our customers can see we're a committed partner. That keeps them from firing us, for the time being.

But when I start to factor in all of these unexpected costs—the tens of thousands of dollars in air shipping, the money spent on repairs and reproduction—I come to understand that our financial statement is much weaker than it appears. Gross margins are nearly halved. And I guess we're not actually in the black. In fact, we're swimming in red ink.

ALWAYS FOCUS ON YOUR "TOTAL DELIVERED COST"

I learned that day that businesses tend to overestimate the savings they will derive from China imports—and underestimate the problems they will encounter. They go in seeking a cheap China cost basis, and get much more than they bargained for in sunk costs, lost time, and disrupted inventory.

There's wisdom in the words of Sam Walton, Wal-Mart's founder, who said he never made much money selling things, but he made a lot of money buying things right. Buying in China is an art, and in large part, it's been the secret to Wal-Mart's success.

If Wal-Mart were a country, it would be China's eighth largest trading partner, importing about $18 billion of goods in 2005.[1] Wal-Mart's global procurement center sits in the southern Chinese city of Shenzhen. It's a honeycomb of buyers whose flintiness is legendary throughout Asia. But just because Wal-Mart imports over 66 percent of its products from China doesn't mean you should import any at all.

Contrary to popular opinion, China is one of the most *expensive* places to do business in the world, unless you know what you're doing. I'm experiencing this cruel lesson firsthand, as the long tail of my business cycle whips around and knocks me on my duff. The problem is that China's commercial and regulatory environments are so complex that any savings you might realize from low labor costs are usually wiped out by supply chain disruptions and legal snares.

I say supply chain. China's supply chain is not really a chain at all. It's more like an ant pile after it's been kicked. Conditions are a mess.

The industries are primitive and fragmented, the roads are bad, the logistics support is worse, and each town has its own particular brand of regulations and dialect. The good news is that China is so complex, it renders foreigners out of the Chinese, as well. If you're from Shenzhen, for example, you're going to have trouble doing business in Ningbo.

To imagine a comparison in the West, you have to go back to the United States before Andrew Carnegie and J. P. Morgan. The flow of goods and materials was a highly messy affair. Low-value firms all along the chain took possession of the product, drawing out lead times and driving up input costs. When the robber barons gobbled up industries like oil and steel and aligned them into vertical monopolies, they were actually rationalizing the flow of goods and materials, making the output more efficient and reliable.

China's industries suffer from bad fragmentation as well, but for different reasons. In the days of communism and the planned economy, Mao wanted each province to be self-sufficient. So most enterprises were duplicated in parallel at the federal, provincial, and municipal levels. This produced a great many redundant and subscale firms. Twenty-five years of market forces have not been enough to shake these useless players out of the chain. Banks have contributed to the problem by financing dubious businesses and spurring overcapacity.

What does that mean for you in-country? It means that a typical supply chain in China has seventeen to twenty-five players! Each supplier that touches the goods will increase costs, risk, and time.

Consider the distribution of plastic resin, as an example. Petrochemicals get formed into plastic pellets by regional producers, like China's Sinopec and Korea's LG, and are sold in bulk to big distributors that supply China's mega-manufacturers. But smaller factories, which make up the lion's share of China's manufacturing base, must buy their lots from subscale middlemen.

In Ningbo, a bustling port near Shanghai, these middlemen sit in

A Typical China Supply Chain

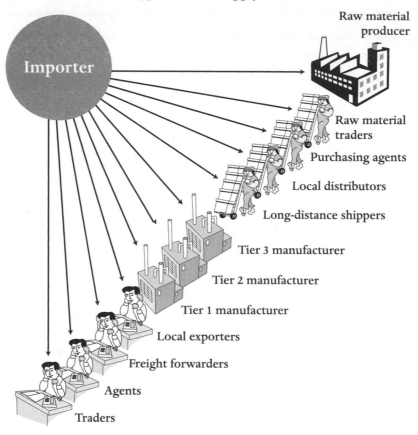

Raw material producer

Raw material traders

Purchasing agents

Local distributors

Long-distance shippers

Tier 3 manufacturer

Tier 2 manufacturer

Tier 1 manufacturer

Local exporters

Freight forwarders

Agents

Traders

cabanas loaded high with resin bags and supplier catalogs. They smoke, yell, and scratch the fluctuating resin prices on sidewalk café chalkboards. They make their money by gaming the dips and spikes in the raw material prices, yet add no value to the product itself. They do increase the cost of goods, though. So before your plastic resin even gets to the factory for processing, your input costs have gone up by 4 to 6 percent or more, just because of the needless participation of these traders.

Fragmentation not only afflicts distribution, it also afflicts the manufacturing base itself. Many factories can perform one function only;

they haven't had the capital to integrate complementary capabilities. For example, an extrusion molder may know how to shoot plastic through a profile but may not have the capability to fabricate the profiles out of steel. So another factory must take care of the design and fabrication of the profiles. And still another must handle the assembly. So a manufacturing program that would require only one supplier in the West often requires multiple suppliers in China.

When a Texas-based maker of specialty automotive parts could not get samples from China that met with their requirements, they went looking to their upstream suppliers for answers. They wanted to make an air conditioner louver for an off-road vehicle, and it should have been a routine, one factory job in the States. Under contract in China were a tool fabricator, an injection molder, and an assembler—all pointing fingers at one another.

Because the job was split among three factories, the program had become more prone to mistakes—and the mistakes were harder to sort out. It took a third-party referee to get the program back on track again. The Texas firm turned to its U.S.-based supply chain service to sort out the mess. They discovered that a subtle but significant flaw in the mold design caused the problem. The design flaw was fixed, and quality-compliant samples were produced.

As the Texas auto parts maker discovered, fragmentation, though widespread, can be circumnavigated. But China's geography, bad infrastructure, and local regulations make the navigating hard. Getting the goods and materials from factory to factory and from factory to port, through different legal jurisdictions, terrain, and states of equipment, is the last thing newcomers tend to think about—but it's a top reason for losing your shirt.

Intra-China logistics will impact your "total delivered cost." Many goods cost 30 to 50 percent more to transport in China than they would in the United States.[2] That's because inland rail moves very slowly and is prone to frequent disruptions—so only goods that can tolerate delays and increased input costs follow this path. To make matters worse, no national trucking network exists yet. The landscape is dominated by mom-and-pops and larger regional carriers, neither of whom urgently care much about meeting your on-time delivery or pickup requirements.

Trucking goods across provinces is also expensive and time-consuming, as trucks are beset with local protectionism, high tolls, and complicated, idiosyncratic licensing requirements. In many cases, trucks cannot enter a new province without a special license. The licenses take many hours to secure, and processing times for "outside" trucks are restricted to certain arbitrary times in the day. Frequently, goods must be loaded into new trucks after hours or days of argument and gesticulation by drivers, bureaucrats, and loaders. I have yet to find a word in Mandarin that quite captures the sense of the English *shakedown,* but the Chinese have mastered this very ancient art.

Most U.S. manufacturers take one of the following three options to navigate China logistics. They contract a Western logistics firm, like FedEx, DHL, UPS, or Ryder, to manage the inbound flow of goods to North America; they contract a large Chinese third-party logistics provider (3PL), such as COSCO, Sinotrans, or China Post; or they build their own logistics network.

In all cases, you need to go under the hood. No single logistics provider controls more than 2 percent market share in China,[3] so even a big player like FedEx is subcontracting most of its inland logistics to smaller players. Make sure to review the capabilities of the subcontractors before starting your import program from China.

Given all of the complexity, you have to wonder why China is the world's manufacturing and assembly hub. It's because of China's highly skilled labor, not because of its cheap labor. There are many countries that can make products more cheaply than China. Most companies keep coming back to China because of quality.

In labor training, China stands supreme. According to the IFC, 84 percent of Chinese firms offer formal training to their labor—compared with the region's 48 percent, and the world's 41 percent. This astonishing trait began with the town and village enterprises, which provided on-the-job training to unskilled workers. Today, most entry-level Chinese engineers—fresh out of college—will already have spent hundreds of hours working different line positions at actual factories.

China also has one of the most nimble manufacturing environments in the world. Unlike South Korea, Taiwan, or Japan, China can turn a program around on a dime. In a world of "just-in-time" manufacturing—where U.S. manufacturers keep costs down by carrying the leanest amount of inventory possible—this capability is critically important.

If you are in the apparel business, for instance, and a fashion trend suddenly changes, in China you can stop a production run mid-cycle, retool, and create a new line of product in time to meet your deadlines. You can't do that anywhere else in the world as nimbly and cost-effectively as you can in China. Though some other Asian nations may attain this level of industrial adroitness (most notably Vietnam), China remains far and away the world's foremost destination for manufacturing and assembly.

Although Americans who do business in China complain that their staff takes every holiday possible—Chinese holidays, American holidays—still, China's work ethic is the stuff of legend. Power permitting, many of China's factories run twenty-four hours a day, in three shifts.

With my factories, however, I have no such luck. I'm finding out that China's famous nimbleness and quality can be elusive—especially if you don't actively manage your factories and course-correct if there are problems. I get on a plane to Shanghai with an Accenture China business consultant at my side, and we conduct a full audit of the business:

the books, the procedures, the documentation, and the factories under contract. Acts of God and forces majeures are one thing. I need to pinpoint what our team is doing to contribute to the problems.

I discover several deficiencies in our organization. Like the fact that we're a lousy matchmaker. Sure, we've inspected and qualified over two thousand factories on the mainland, yet it seems we can't hire the right factories for the jobs we've got. A school supplies factory is making a precision medical device for us. A lightbulb factory is making a pump.

Kickbacks? Possibly. But more likely just incompetence. Or worse: bad organizational structure. We have three unsupervised staffers responsible for selecting factories. On paper, they are all reporting to my partner in New York. But six thousand miles away, they have pretty much a free hand. These guys are all good engineers but lack purchasing experience and have no direct supervisor to help them appraise suppliers.

They're also just overwhelmed. Each day, we are working on dozens of projects—many of them in the quotation phase. So they must toil round-the-clock scouring the countryside for factories and are having trouble keeping up.

Lack of supervision is also impairing our ability to execute well on orders. Because there's no local oversight, our project engineers are adrift. They're interfacing with the factories every day, and they come to see themselves more as the advocates of the factory than the advocates of our customers. Big problem. When factories are lying to us that orders are proceding apace, our engineers are parroting the plant managers' words to us at headquarters, and we're believing them.

Many entrepreneurs claim that the road to success is never a straight line. In China, you can take that advice to the bank. Here we've got a book of growing orders, new business leads coming in every week, and a team that is not up to the task of executing on our business model.

We've already punted once. Now we must punt again. The organization has to be overhauled. Without disrupting our book of ongoing orders. Heaven help us.

HOW TO BEGIN?

I'd spend the coming years striving to build a company that was up to the challenges in China. Today, with the benefit of hindsight, when I'm helping clients figure out how to import, I begin by asking three questions:

1. Does China make what you need?
2. Do the economics make sense?
3. What are your business objectives?

Does China Make What You Need?

China is getting adept at making more advanced products. The question is whether these products can meet Western tolerances. A great many firms in China serve local markets, and you will find huge disparities in the product specifications and quality standards between China and the West—in everything from how many BTUs the air-conditioning equipment must generate to how many times a doorknob can be turned before it breaks. I never knew that if you turn a typical Chinese doorknob one thousand times, it will probably break. To break a typical American doorknob, you've got to turn it ten thousand times.

Standards often differ by an order of magnitude, as with the doorknobs. Sometimes prices do too. Most manufacturing programs begin with a tooling phase. You'll be happy to hear the price differential between Western and Chinese tools is startling. It's often a tenfold difference. A tool that may cost $200,000 in the United States may cost $20,000 or less in China.

There are many reasons for this. One reason, most notably, is labor cost. The costs of steel are about the same in China, if not more, so you're not saving on raw materials. You're saving on all the labor required to design and fabricate a mold, which is literally sculpted out of steel.

Also, there's a key difference in what you're getting for your money—and this is where most buyers get hamstrung. After a successful production run, a Florida boating retailer chose to have their mold shipped over from China. The products that came off the mold looked great. But the mold itself was a mess. Inferior steel, kludge construction, caked in grime. The importer was horrified.

If you don't specify in advance that you plan on taking possession of your tool after the program, then a Chinese factory will usually build a tool that fulfills the minimum production requirements, but might not live up to accepted engineering standards. Progressive dies in the West, for instance, are complex, multifaceted machines that automatically move a part through a number of individual dies. In China, a progressive die usually consists of a group of individual line dies, requiring a laborer to feed the part from tool to tool.

It's not a matter of insufficient know-how. Good Chinese factories can usually build a progressive die to suit Western standards. But if the tool is not earmarked for export, the factory will choose to use cheaper (and often proprietary) methods to get the job done.

If you terminate your program—and you didn't originally order your tool "to go"—the factory will almost always resist handing it over to you. It doesn't matter that you paid for the tool, and that it's your property on paper. The factory owner will insist that the mold was priced to remain on the shop floor. If you want your mold for export, you'll need to pay more—sometimes much more.

Smart U.S. importers take advantage of this situation. They produce two molds for each program: a dirt-cheap "domestic" mold to make parts in the Chinese factory, as well as an inexpensive export mold, to be shipped to the U.S. plant, should further runs need to be made onshore.

Bearing in mind that both product standards and what you get for your money can differ widely from what you'd expect in the United States, there are various ways to determine whether China makes what you need. Many people choose to apply a simple rule of thumb: if the job requires a lot of direct labor, China can make it cheaper. But that's not always true. You need to know whether the labor is skilled enough to make products that are up to your requirements.

Skills vary widely in China—from city to city, even from factory to factory. In general, each city has its own areas of specialization. When considering if China makes what you need, do some homework on China's industrial cities. Each has trade fairs and Web sites.* Here are some of the main ones:

Chengdu

In the province of Sichuan, Chengdu is the financial and information technology hub of southwestern China, but transportation from Chengdu to the nearest seaport takes seven to ten days. There is also currently a shortage of cargo containers, and there are no regular flights for large cargo planes. Still, Sichuan Province is now home to more than five thousand foreign-funded enterprises, because of tax breaks and other perks offered to companies investing there. Over thirty large multinational corporations, including Motorola, PepsiCo, Coca-Cola, and McDonnell Douglas of the United States, Chit Tat of Thailand, Bayer and Siemens of Germany, and Toyota and Mitsubishi of Japan, have started operations in Sichuan. Key industries are IT, machinery, metallurgy, pharmaceuticals, chemicals, food and beverage, and building materials.[4]

*For maps, city descriptions, and city trade fares, visit AllTheT.com/cities.

Dalian

Dalian was occupied by the Russians, then the Japanese. It returned to Chinese rule in 1949, having received the benefit of advanced infrastructure and technology. Since 1980, the city's economic development has been bankrolled by the likes of Hewlett Packard, General Electric, IBM, and Microsoft.

Dalian is China's second-largest seaport, after Shanghai. The Dalian International Airport offers the largest air cargo terminal in northeast China and is capable of handling domestic and international cargo. Key industries include food processing, machinery, IT, electronics, garments, petrochemicals, household goods, textiles, locomotives, shipbuilding, pharmaceuticals, chemicals, and petroleum refining. Key agricultural products include grain, corn, sorghum, cotton, soybeans, sea cucumber, fish, prawns, abalone, apples, grapes, peaches, and cherries.

Hangzhou

The capital of Zhejiang Province, Hangzhou sits on a bay but lacks a port, so goods must be hauled to Shanghai or Ningbo for shipment (about a four-hour drive, depending on road conditions). Feasibility studies for port development are in the works. Key industries include machinery, electronics, information technology, pharmaceuticals, chemicals, textiles (especially silk and cotton), and food and beverage processing.

Harbin

Harbin was a small fishing village in the nineteenth century and became a mainstay of China's old command economy. It was featured as one of the key cities during the nation's first Five Year Plan. Harbin has an inland port, rail access to Beijing, and good airport infrastructure. By end of year 2001, there were 581 foreign-funded enterprises in the development zone. Yet in 2004, 70 percent of production remained in the hands of the state—in comparison to 20 percent in Guangdong Province. Harbin excels in the following industries: textiles, medicine, foodstuffs, automotive, metallurgy, electronics, building materials, and chemicals.

Nanjing

Capital of Jiangsu Province, Nanjing is one of China's fastest-growing cities economically (in 2004, its GDP increased 17 percent). It was also ranked eighth in *Forbes'* list of Chinese cities most favorable for business. Nanjing boasts the largest inland river port in Asia and has good rail, roads, and air links. Over one thousand American companies are already doing business in Nanjing. Its key industries include petrochemicals and steel, but it is increasingly becoming an important manufacturing base for high-technology goods such as electronics, advanced materials, and biotech. Leading products include software, flat panel displays, auto parts, precision instruments, ethylene, and acetic acid.

Ningbo

Ningbo runs a major deepwater port and has a cargo throughput of more than 100 million tons. Railways connect with Xiaoshan, Shanghai, and Zheliang. The airport links directly with Hong Kong, Macao, and Shanghai. It is estimated that there are 62,500 private enterprises in Ningbo. Key industries include machinery, housewares, electronics, and large-scale harbor-based industries represented by petrochemicals, iron and steel, power generation, and paper making. Up-and-coming industries include biotech, electronics, and IT.

Qingdao

Qingdao is another thriving port city on China's eastern seaboard. In the past twenty years, Qingdao has attracted over $19 billion in foreign direct investment, with over 17,854 foreign-invested companies. Seventy-six Fortune 500 companies have established projects in Qingdao. Key industries include automobiles, consumer electronics, building materials, shipbuilding, petrochemicals, steel, beer and wine, textiles and apparel, food processing equipment, and chemical fertilizer. Qingdao's Shandong Province is rich in mineral resources and crude oil (representing 15 percent of the country's total). The soil contains sulphur, diamonds, graphite, coal, iron, and magnetite.

Shanghai

In this city of 7.5 million people, the customs officials work twenty-four hours a day, seven days a week. Shanghai is also the nation's financial center. At the end of 2004, there were 113 foreign financial institutions operating in Shanghai. Foreign investments in Shanghai are mainly engaged in industry (62.4 percent of foreign direct investment from 1979 to 2004 has gone into manufacturing). Key industries include automobiles, petrochemicals, specialty chemicals, steel and iron, biotech, electronics, textiles, and IT. Consumer goods manufactured include specialized dies, lathes, electronic assembly equipment, watches, cameras, radios, fountain pens, glassware, leather goods, stationery products, and hardware.

Shenzhen

There are twelve ports in Shenzhen, including the world's fourth-largest container port. Guangdong Province has a strong private sector; it is the birthplace of China's marketplace. Production by the private sector (non-state-owned and non-state-holding enterprises) accounted for 83 percent of the province's total industrial output. Key industries include high-tech products (especially mobile phones), electric machinery, metals, medical equipment, pharmaceuticals, food processing, textiles, apparel, chemicals, plastics, and transportation equipment. Here is a partial list of the foreign companies already doing business in Shenzhen: Mitsui, Mitsubishi, Sanyo, Panasonic, Toshiba, Sony, Squibb, Harris, Du Pont, Siemens, Lufthansa, ING, HP-Compaq, Carrefour, Lucent, PepsiCo, Whirlpool, Kodak, McDonald's, AIG, Citigroup, Philip Morris Companies, Johnson Controls, Sears, FedEx, Sara Lee, HSBC, ABN AMRO, IBM—oh, and Wal-Mart.

Tianjin

Known as a heavy industrial base for northeast China, Tianjin's barriers to entry against SMEs are unique: there is a $200,000 minimum capital requirement, which inhibits smaller firms from entering the market. That being said, Tianjin is an export processing center for a wide range of products. Key industries include automobiles, electronics, petrochemical products, metallurgy, medicine, mechanical industries, and new energy sources. Other industries include advanced building materials, plastic products, consumer durables, and food and beverage packaging. Foreign-invested enterprises account for 49 percent of gross industrial output.

Wuhan

Capital of Hubei Province, Wuhan is billed as the crossroads to nine provinces. It's a port city on the Yangtze and Hanshui rivers, and hosts an estimated thirty thousand manufacturing and high-tech firms. Key industries include photo electronics, automobiles, steel and iron, and biotech. Other emerging industries in Wuhan include metallurgy, textiles, food products, heavy machinery, glass, cement, fertilizer, electronics, packaging, and printing.

Xiamen

Located in Fujian Province (across the straits from Taiwan), Xiamen is a regional transportation hub, distributing everything from minerals and textiles to wood pulp, paper, electrical and mechanical products, chemicals, and base metals. Approximately six thousand foreign-invested

enterprises have established a presence in Xiamen, many of them Taiwanese. Xiamen imports (from the United States) aircraft parts, plastics, machinery, electronic products, steel, and agricultural products.
Key industries include electronics, machinery, and chemicals. Other
emerging industries include pharmaceuticals, textiles, foodstuffs, and
building materials.

If you find that a Chinese city makes what you need in general, you
can drill down and determine whether any suppliers make your product specifically. Some of this legwork can be done on the Web, but the
best way is to hop on a plane and visit. Go to one of the many trade
fairs that will be featured for your industry in China, and start meeting
some of these people firsthand.

Do the Economics Make Sense?

In analyzing the economics of a China import program, direct labor
costs are usually the first thing people think about, but they really
ought to be the last.

Start, instead, with your firm's value proposition. Define your competitive advantage in each product line. Use operational metrics such
as speed to market, your manufacturing costs, and inventory holding
costs. Then assess your tolerance for risk: the relative costs of inventory disruptions, stolen intellectual property, and compromised product integrity. If your company has a track record for product reliability
and speed, you need to think carefully about the risks you will encounter in China and how to manage them.

Then consider your direct labor costs. For many industries in the
West, direct labor is declining because of investments in technology. If
direct labor costs are already low, sourcing product from China may
kill your margins and your competitive advantage through unforeseen
costs and disruptions. If labor represents 40 to 50 percent of your cost
of goods, you should seriously consider importing. For industries with
stable, predictable demand, low inventory holding costs, and high

direct labor costs, sourcing product from China probably makes good sense.

Finally, you should factor in shipping costs. Some products lend themselves very well to shipping, others do not. You should try to use as much of the space inside your container as possible. Every inch of air is money you lose. If your products nest together, that's one good sign that they will lend themselves well to shipping.

But if the goods are very heavy—like granite countertops, for instance—you may max out the weight of the container and must consider shipping as a major contributor to your total delivered cost. Aside from weight, there's also the issue of volume. One client of mine wanted to ship giant slabs of Styrofoam. They were very light and nested well, but took up so much room in the cube that we needed hundreds of sea containers to fulfill the order. The economics just didn't make sense when you compared the cost to local sources.

In addition to considering the costs to make and ship your product, you also need to analyze start-up costs. As in any foreign country, in China, it's going to cost you something to get your program set up—and that cost may be prohibitively expensive, depending on your business goals. The good news is that today, sourcing firms and third-party agents will often import discrete items for you without too much in the way of down payments. But you should be aware that for every project, there's an entry fee. If you're just sticking your toe in the water, make sure that's all you're sticking in.

What Are My Business Objectives?

If China makes what you need, and if the economics make sense and the setup costs are not too high, you can get down to business. You don't need to think in terms of sending all of your production overseas, or "outsourcing your shop." Savvy businesses today think in terms of discrete business goals and how China imports can support them.

Attack Adjacent Markets

One way to use China imports is to attack new or adjacent markets. A Toledo-based food service company put this strategy to the test. Already the market leader in glass food service products, now they wanted to enter the market for plastic goods. They'd be going head-to-head with some big established competitors in the space, though.

The Toledo firm was betting they could use their market share in glass—and the advantage of their broad installed customer base—to cross-sell plastics. But this was just a hunch, and senior management was reluctant to invest in plant and equipment before testing whether they could compete in this new market.

It was a strategy with some risks. Many of the markets the company was seeking to enter allowed slim margins at best. Plastic cups and tumblers, spatulas, mixing spoons, and the like, these products required minimal labor to make. They were essentially "commodity" products—the raw material cost would make up most of the total cost of goods. The key to success on the supply side of this formula, then, was to buy the raw materials at the right price, then manufacture and import as cost-efficiently as possible. They needed to come in at least at the same price as their competition, if not lower. So there was a slim margin for error.

Though the Toledo firm had sourced glass products from China for many years, they were not staffed to handle plastics. So they chose to hire a U.S. sourcing firm to help them screen and select China factories, then run the manufacturing.

The sourcing firm had a staff in China that did some gumshoeing. They wanted to find out which factories the competitors were contracting. Often, factories will create competitive products in the same shop. So an athletic bag maker will be stamping Nike on one bag and Adidas on another, but they're essentially the same bag. The sourcing firm was trying to determine whether the competitors' factories might produce goods for the Toledo firm, as well.

Though that route proved helpful in providing competitive intelligence, the factories were already very busy making goods for the competition. Taking on additional work was not appealing to them—especially as the Toledo firm could not realistically forecast the volume of goods they'd need for the coming years.

Many of China's factories are humming with business, so usually, they need to be pitched on the business potential of your partnership. They must invest in personnel, equipment, and raw materials to ramp up for your production run, and most China factories have been burned many, many times by Western buyers who pit a group of factories against each other to create first article samples, only to stiff the losing factories on payment. Chinese suppliers, therefore, are often leery of new business and will not always jump at the opportunity to make your goods.

The sourcing firm cut good deals on the raw materials, contracted competent factories, and produced the goods with relatively little pain or disruption. But the Toledo firm encountered stiff resistance in the marketplace to their plastic product line extensions. Some customers bought, but most of them stayed with the competition.

The Toledo food service company maintains its beachhead in plastics. It is steadily clawing market share away from the competition, and continues to use China sourcing to achieve this discrete business goal.

Extend Core Business Lines

Other U.S. firms import goods from China to deepen or widen their core offering. One good example is Cavalier Homes in Alabama. Cavalier is a midsized publicly listed company that makes manufactured homes—homes that are built on an assembly line, then trucked to the site on a large flatbed. This type of house used to be known as a "mobile home," a term the industry prefers not to use. Today's typical manufactured homes look, feel, and last like a real house.

There are thousands of different individual products that go into one of these houses—the plumbing, the electrical, the heating and ventilation, the appliances, the furniture, the tchotchkes. Now multiply that list by dozens of different floor plans and home models, all requiring different products SKUs—fifteen-inch Venetian blinds in Model A, seventeen-inch Venetian blinds in Model B, and on and on, all the way through the product list.

The buyer is tasked with handling this dizzying array of thousands of products: purchasing them at the right price, certainly, but also managing the inventory levels. If Model A stops selling, you can't put the fifteen-inch Venetian blinds into another floor plan. They won't fit. So in addition to complexity, you've got a problem with obsolescence.

Cavalier used China sourcing to streamline their product mix, boost their margins, and outwit the competition.

First, Cavalier's purchasing manager worked with the home designers to standardize as many elements as possible, without compromising product quality. What could be readily sourced from China played a big role in determining what products were adopted for the new, standardized floor plans. In so doing, they slimmed the product list from over ten thousand to under two. This would simplify purchasing and make it much easier to manage inventory and obsolescence.

After streamlining what they purchased, they analyzed *how* they purchased. At the time, Cavalier worked primarily with local and regional distributors, who imported a lot of their goods from China.

But Cavalier understood that local suppliers, though well-intentioned and smart, might not be extracting the most value out of their China sources. Indeed, there is often a long chain of intermediaries between a local distributor, say, in Phil Campbell, Alabama, and the China source in Shenzhen. Often the local distributor will work with an importer. The importer, in turn, will work through a trading company, which (if it's Taiwanese or Japanese) might work through still another trading company (probably Chinese) before the actual China factories are reached.

Each one of those players adds to the input cost without providing much value. They also make the lead time longer and the program riskier. Cavalier wanted to help their local suppliers buy smarter, by disintermediating any unnecessary players in the chain. They enlisted a U.S. sourcing firm to help.

Cavalier would dictate which products their local suppliers would buy, and the suppliers, in turn, would issue the purchase orders to the sourcing firm. That way, the local distributors would not be cut out, but low-value players upstream would.

The test worked. The products looked great, were compliant with U.S. regs, and saved Cavalier significant money—over 25 percent on some items, more on others. The buyer was delighted to learn that even on commodity items like valves and fittings, there was still room to save more money by cutting out unnecessary intermediaries.

While the competition was spending millions of dollars with the Big Three consulting firms trying to streamline their product lists through large systems integration projects, Cavalier got the job done with their local suppliers and a good China sourcing firm.

Defend Low Price Points from Competition

Here's a little corporate kung fu: using China to compete with China. Savvy companies today are importing goods from China to defend their markets from Chinese competition. A midsized Long Island wholesaler of medical and dental supplies was facing Chinese heat on its low-priced products—the "film mounts" that dentists slip their tiny X-ray photos into, before they're placed on the backlit screen. In order to defend these product lines, the wholesaler turned to a U.S.-based China sourcing firm.

These products look pretty simple, but they actually require three different manufacturing processes. The paper and plastic sheets must be rolled, then stamped, then printed with the client's logo. They might not require the precision of surgical equipment, but they definitely require competence on the part of the factory.

It took the sourcing firm some time to get their bearings. They hadn't produced this kind of product before, and had to go searching for factories. They bid out the job among five suppliers, and were enticed by the especially low price point of one particular China shop.

The reason the price point was so low was that the factory intended to use human stampers instead of machines to save money and free up their stamping machines for other jobs. Linemen took the large sheets of rolled paper and plastic and cut them by hand out of stencils with large knives. This technique was slow and rife with human error. First articles did not pass inspection. Neither did the second batch. Or the third. Finally, the sourcing firm realized they had enlisted the wrong sort of supplier and turned to slightly higher-priced, but competent, firms that had the necessary equipment and trained personnel to make the film mounts according to client specifications.

Despite losing some time, the Long Island importer was able to keep its current customers in tow by offering them "China prices" that matched or beat their Chinese competitors. If you're feeling the heat of Chinese competition, consider importing from China as a line of defense.

Launch a New Business

Other firms turn to China imports to bootstrap a new business—like the start-up that designed a unique product for the marine industry. Until now, chumming had always been done, by commercial and recreational fishermen alike, by punching holes in a ziplock bag. Chum King, LLC, had invented a product that was superior to the ziplock bag in many ways. First, it was weighted, so it sank; and it was a lot cleaner than a ziplock. The chum would sit in a chamber that could either be locked in place, or slide open and shut with the current. Nothing like this existed in the marketplace, and the founders of the company—fishermen both—knew that if they could bring this product to market cost-efficiently, they'd have a winner.

Some China sourcing firms go beyond just buying goods off the shelves of local factories. They have the ability to design and prototype new products; they can take a sample and reverse-engineer it, or take specs and build a new prototype. Chum King turned to such a firm. The partnership proved valuable, as the China partner started making good engineering suggestions on how the product design could be improved. After the design revisions, the product would be stronger and cost less.

Once prototypes of the product were made, Chum King exhibited their wares at the major East Coast marine trade shows and worked the floor, meeting with as many distributors as they could. The buyers liked what they saw, and they started placing trial orders.

Chum King cut a purchase order for a full container load of the product—about six thousand units—from its China partner and had them shipped to a warehouse in Florida. After the products arrived, it occurred to the owners that they should include a small clip with each product, to enable the user to fasten the chamber shut. Each bag had to be opened and a clip inserted. In handling every single product over the course of the next several months, the owners at Chum King were amazed that they could spot zero defects. Normally, a given batch of manufactured goods will have a certain percentage of defective units. The question then becomes whether the defects fall within the acceptable quality limits of the product. Some level of defects is usually tolerated in product specifications. All six thousand products were eventually sold. Not one had a defect, not one was returned by a customer.

As the demand in the marketplace was established, and relationships cemented with distributors up and down the coast, Chum King began to work with their China sourcing partner to import smaller batches, shipped to warehouses in Long Island, North Carolina, and Florida. That way, the product inventories were closer to Chum King's customers, saving money and time on transportation.

Chum King continues to lead the market and still relies on the same China sourcing partner to manage its manufacturing and export.

Once you've determined whether China makes what you need, whether the economics make sense on your order, and whether your China sourcing program supports a specific business objective, it's time to think about how to approach the market.

Should you go through a middleman or go direct to Chinese sources? You'll encounter many kinds of middlemen in the marketplace: sourcing firms, third party logistics providers (3PL), importers, agents, and even Internet portals.

There are some advantages to using a middleman. One is the relatively low cost of entry. This way, you can experiment before having to commit significant dollars and personnel. Another advantage is flexibility. If one hypothesis doesn't pan out (say, the product you import doesn't sell), you can nimbly switch in midstream and try something new. A final advantage—and this is a benefit especially to small firms— is the ability to order à la carte.

Let's say you sell a mixed product line. You don't have tremendous sales volume, and you need different amounts of each item. To set up that operation in China would be a complex, costly job. But by working through a competent intermediary that is the right fit with your business, you can tailor your importing to your needs: one thousand units of one item, three thousand of another, fifty-five thousand of another—packed as "mixed batches" in sea containers, and delivered to your warehouse or your distributor.

By ordering only what you need, you speed up your inventory turns and keep your business lean. In imports, "lean" is much more than just a buzzword. It's an essential business posture. When you embark on an import program, you are managing working capital in motion. The longer your supply chain, the costlier the final delivered cost—and the greater the chance for disruption.

So there are advantages to using an intermediary. However, there are some drawbacks, as well. The number of China middlemen has ballooned over recent years. A simple Internet search for "China sourcing" will reveal hundreds. Unfortunately, these firms vary widely, and many deliver substandard service and defective product.

THE SEVEN STEPS TO A SUCCESSFUL IMPORT PROGRAM

I can't count all the frustrated companies that have come to me after being burned by an intermediary. Follow these seven steps to manage a smooth, profitable import program.

Step One: Do Your Due Diligence

Most U.S. buyers cite suppliers and logistics as the main causes of costly disruptions. In both cases, smaller businesses can learn a lot from Wal-Mart, who wrote the book on China sourcing.

Wal-Mart invests a lot of time and energy before an import program begins in order to minimize issues down the road. At the onset of every import program they conduct an investigatory phase. You should do the same. How involved this phase gets depends on whether you've done business with your supplier before. If this is a new relationship, you've got a lot of due diligence to do. Your due diligence should include pricing, samples, and plant appraisal.

A typical importing program will begin with a request for quotation, in which you inform your supplier candidates what you want to make, how much, and when you need it by. Some suppliers will charge you a fee to provide you a price quotation. That is to ward away window shoppers—or buyers who are merely seeking a comparative quote in order to justify their current pricing.

Remember that putting together a good quotation takes time and resources from your supplier, so if you are asking them to quote on an item with multiple parts, don't be surprised if they request a fee. This, of course, is negotiable.

Once you get your price quotes, it's important that you break these down. Good cost modeling is imperative. Pricing is a window onto your supplier: how competent they are, how greedy. Unless you have a sense of how your factories are charging you, you won't be able to determine (a) whether they can successfully do the job, and (b) whether they can make a margin that supports their liquidity needs.

Many suppliers will try to quote rock-bottom prices in an effort to lure your business—prices so low that they will lose money on the engagement. Others will quote the business at a zero margin, just to win your business, then hike up their prices down the line.

To spot these pitfalls ahead of time, here is a good cost model I often employ. Find out numbers to accompany each of the following categories:

Cost Model

Raw materials:
    Unit price
    Usage
    Waste
Cycle time
Profit margin
Tax

You can back into the profit margin number, once you know the other variables. As a rule, it's a good idea to allow the factory a decent—though not exorbitant—margin. First, it will significantly reduce the chances that the factory will try to screw you. Second, it builds good faith in the working relationship. And third, it gives you room to tamp down, over time.

This is a technique employed with great skill by Wal-Mart, and savvy smaller firms today are following suit. Once dependable volumes have been established with your suppliers, and you've done some business together, you can begin to sit on the profit margins all the way along the chain—from raw materials to manufacturing and even shipping. Of course, the higher your volume, the more you can tamp down. But even smaller, but predictable, volumes will allow you some leverage in negotiating a drop in price. (Your customer will probably be sitting on *your* margins over time, as well.)

Once you've compared prices among the bidding factories, you need to take into consideration the quality of their samples. If you are in an industry that requires compliance with regs, such as medical supplies, you should have your samples tested by a third-party lab. This is usually not too costly, and will save you heartache down the road.

Good supplier appraisal is also imperative, which should include an on-site plant assessment and a review of the supplier's quality procedures. If you contract a middleman, make sure you appraise the subcontractors. I can't tell you how many companies have come to me after trusting factories from an Internet middleman, like Alibaba.com, sight unseen. The more work you do up front in determining the strengths and weaknesses of your suppliers, the more disruptions and costly mistakes you will avoid down the line.

Step Two: Reach Out to a Customs Broker

Logistics are not something to consider at the end of your program, when it's time for the goods to ship. If you've waited until then, you're too late. Logistics need to be planned at the beginning of the program, as you're setting everything up. They're a key factor in your costing and scheduling.

Many midsized firms have their own logistics department. If you don't, I'd recommend getting in touch with a freight forwarder. There are maritime forwarders and air cargo forwarders. The services they provide include quoting ocean or air freight rates; quoting truck, rail, or other freight rates for services needed to move shipments to and from the port; making arrangements for the transportation; and preparing documents needed for international shipping.

Some freight forwarders are also customs brokers. A customs broker is an essential person in your import program. A true customs broker must be licensed under very strict standards by the Customs Service of the U.S. Treasury Department. The customs broker is in charge of collecting the exact duty amounts and handing them over to the government. A customs broker is not the same as an import broker, who buys and sells goods for resale. In order for a firm to operate as a customs broker in a particular city, there must be a licensed broker present on the premises. Many firms provide a mix of these three services: ocean and air freight forwarding and customer brokerage.

Get in touch with a handful of freight forwarders in your area. You'll find there are many, some with offices all over the world, and some with just a local storefront. Make an appointment and go down and visit the forwarder. Get a sense of what their offices are like, and whether you feel comfortable working with their staff.

Unless you already have a specific customer that is considering placing an order with you, don't get too specific about your plans. Without an order in hand, you will just be wasting the forwarder's time if you ask them to provide you with quotes. You can talk instead about the type of product you are looking to import and what part of the world it's coming from, your documentation requirements, and even price lists.

As an importer, you should be aware that with "CIF" quotations (cost, insurance, and freight included), your forwarder is arranging for your insurance, plus charging you for it. If you get a CIF quotation, comparison-shop. Request quotations that compare the CIF price with an FOB price ("free on board" vessel), which is the price of loading the goods onto the ship, but not transporting them. That'll give you an idea of what your forwarder or importer is marking up.

Step Three: Set Up Financing

Now that you have samples in hand, a cost model, and an idea of how you're going to transport the goods, you need to set up how you're going to pay for the program. If you're financing the order yourself, there are a variety of ways to fund imports that don't require you to put your hand too deeply into your pocket, if at all. Banks, factors, and even logistics firms can help.

Chances are, your bank has an international department. If not, you don't need to switch your checking account to your international banker. (Though some documents will need to be transferred from bank to bank.)

Visit your international banker and explain your program: what you're planning to import, how you are planning to forward the freight. Ask what international services they offer. They should be able to provide you with an array of financing options—from letters of credit to international money wires. They should also be able to provide you with a list of fees.

In terms of funding your order, your bank may also provide assistance. If you have a long-standing relationship with them, they may write a letter of credit for you to purchase goods, without escrowing the money in your account.

However, if your bank won't finance you, and you need alternative sources of funding, there are factors and even logistics companies. Factors finance your "net" period—from the time your customer takes receipt of the goods until the time required to pay. A factor usually charges very high rates for this financing, often as high as 40 percent annualized. But the time period to be financed is typically thirty, sixty, or ninety days. A factor may be an option for you if you are on an open account with *your* customer, and must wait a specified period to get paid (and in turn, pay your factory).

Logistics companies also provide financing solutions. UPS, for example, has a division called UPS Capital, which is specifically devoted to helping small businesses finance trade. Also, many financial services firms have begun offering trade and project finance, such as CIT and Pacific Life.

Finally, you should investigate the many U.S. government resources that can help you. The Export-Import Bank of the United States is a good place to start.*

Step Four: Set Commercial, Engineering, and Regulatory Terms

Your purchase order (PO) is the primary working document and contract between you and your supplier. Clarify all important terms in advance—commercial, engineering, regulatory, and documentary—to ensure that you and your supplier understand one another; and also so that all terms can be clearly referenced in the PO, so that they, in effect, become contractually binding.

Commercial Terms

There are four standard payment types in international trade, each with its own financing implications attached to it. From most to least advantageous to the importer, they are: open account, draft (time or sight), letter of credit (time or sight), and prepayment.

MOST ADVANTAGEOUS: OPEN ACCOUNT. In this scenario, you pay nothing until a specified period elapses *after you take receipt of goods.* Meaning that you receive the goods and the documents, and then the clock starts ticking on your payable. Typical open account terms are 30 days, 60 days, and even 120 days. This is often called the net payment term (as in "net 30, net 60, or net 120").

---

*For a guide to government resources, visit AllTheT.com/resources.

NEXT-TO-MOST ADVANTAGEOUS: DRAFT. With a sight draft, you don't have the protections afforded you by a letter of credit. However, you're more protected than with an open account. People sometimes refer to draft payment as a "letter of credit without a letter of credit." This method should be considered if you have some trust with your supplier but are not ready for an open account payment term.

NEXT-TO-LEAST ADVANTAGEOUS, BUT STILL GOOD: LETTER OF CREDIT. This financial instrument has been used for hundreds of years and has evolved to provide maximum protections for the buyer and the seller. The banks take the place of importer and exporter in handling the documents and monies. It should be underscored, though, that a letter of credit is not a guarantee that you will be paid. A letter of credit is simply a guarantee that the buyer's bank will pay, as long as the terms in the letter are complied with exactly. A single mistake, and payment is optional.

Here's a tip. You want your shipping documents to arrive before the goods do. Use this language in your letter of credit to make sure that happens:

Beneficiary must present a certificate that he has:

1. Sent a fax to the applicant with
   a. Name of vessel
   b. Sailing date
   c. Estimated arrival date and port
   d. Bill of lading number, and
2. Sent to the applicant by airmail a copy of each and every document submitted under this letter of credit (photocopies acceptable).

If you're using air cargo, you should especially remember to make this documentary request, as the goods will always precede the documents. When the document copies arrive, pass them on to your customs broker.

LEAST ADVANTAGEOUS: PREPAYMENT. Chinese factories will invariably ask for this payment option first. They want cash money down on the order before they start production, and the balance to be paid before the goods leave the port. You'll negotiate. A letter of credit is a good way to meet in the middle.

Engineering Terms

Agree upon one set of design and product specifications, and reference these specifications in the purchase order. If changes are made to the terms, make sure the PO is amended to reference any new specs or requirements. Similar up-front effort needs to be put into benchmarking and preparing for your quality control and on-time delivery requirements. It's often a good idea to reference these in the PO, as well.

Regulatory Terms

Make sure you are familiar with the regs that apply to your import—and that your supplier is as well. Many products are regulated by different standards bodies. If you don't know the regulations that apply to your product, go online and find out. Type in your product name in a search engine, along with the terms "standards" and "regulations," and see what you find. If you need help, talk to your customs broker. Make sure to reference the regulations in the PO.*

Step Five: Obtain as Many Buying Commitments as Possible before Importing

Easier said than done, I know. But there are companies like College Comfort, LLC, of North Carolina that are so synchronized with their China supplier that they can book orders in advance of buying raw

*For more about commercial, engineering, and regulatory terms, visit AllTheT.com/terms.

material and committing production resources. They had to go through a season or two first of ironing out the kinks, though.

Another way to try to secure as many sales as possible before committing dollars is through test-marketing your product in a small area, then rolling it out if it sells. Retailers that use TV infomercials to drive phone and Internet sales use this technique to great effect. They line up China suppliers, have samples made, then produce a low-budget commercial or a more lengthy infomercial, if they have deep pockets.

They'll cut "per inquiry deals" with the television media—meaning that the TV affiliates will be paid with each lead generated or product sold. Usually, the TV station will run the commercial in remnant ad space, such as late at night on the weekend—which happens to be precisely the time when most people are biting their cuticles thinking about how they're going to pay their credit card bills—and are *buying* from infomercials.

The retailer will tell you to allow four to six weeks to delivery, because they'll wait until they've received a minimum number of orders before they start production. Then, they'll have the factories run night and day for a few days, and put the goods on a ship that will arrive in the States five weeks later, to be sent on to your address from a mail-sorting center. If a product tanks, they'll run a small batch, and try something new.

Step Six: Monitor Documentation, Cash, and Time Flows

After the program begins, it's not time to sit back and wait for the goods to arrive. It's time to manage the trajectory of the order. If you're working with an intermediary, it's time to ride herd, ensuring that they are crossing all the T's and dotting all the I's. If you are working directly with a factory, you'll need to act as the last line of defense for quality control.

In any given program, there are three elements you'll need to monitor and manage: cash, information, and time.

Managing the Cash-to-Cash Cycle

The difference between making money and losing money on an import program depends on how well you manage the phases of cash commitments.

A good idea is to map out these commitments so you can track them throughout the order. Here is an example of how accounts payable are tracked through the manufacturing and logistics phases of a program. This flow chart features documents and activities associated with those documents. If you're managing a team, this sort of map will coordinate what needs to happen when each cash-related document is received.

Your version of events will probably be different, but illustrating them clearly will help you manage each step. I have heard many horror stories about how a single step in this process was delayed or forgotten—and how that meant the difference between profit and loss.

PAYMENT FLOW

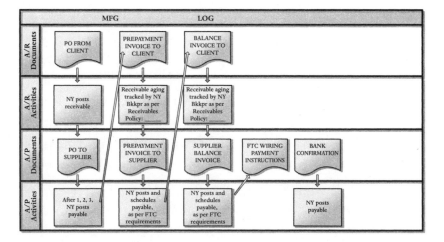

Managing Information

If you're a small business, the thorniest aspect of importing may very well be the documentation. Many small businesses complain that they get hamstrung over this.

There are three kinds of documents you'll need to keep track of: cash related, project related, and shipping related. Mapping out each track before a program begins is the best way to make sure you don't get flummoxed. Build a job jacket for each program, containing all the documents.

If you went ahead and mapped out your cash-to-cash commitments above, then you'll have a list of cash-related documents. That's your first track. Next, move on to project- and shipping-related documents.

Here is a typical list of the documents you will encounter, and their key elements:

Request for Quotation
    Design specs
    Material specs
    Inspection methodology
    Packaging requirements
    Product drawings
    Dimensions
    Volume

Supplier Bids
    Bid conforms to specs
    Supplier recommendation
    Evaluation sheets
        Equipment
        Capacity
        QC
        Personnel

Quotation

    Per client/ spec #_____

    Per client sample _____

    Note nonconformance with spec, as necessary:

    Cost model audit

    Client feedback:

    Revision 1:

    Revision 2:

    Revision 3:

Client Purchase Order

    Pricing corresponds with quote?

    Terms correspond with quote?

    Delivery date corresponds with quote?

    Quantity corresponds with quote?

    Specification reference #_____

Purchase Order to Supplier

    Description references quote and client PO

    Pricing ($/RMB) conforms with quote, PO, and bid

    Terms conform with quote and PO

    Quantity conforms with quote and PO

    Delivery date conforms with quote and PO

    References to client/ spec #_____

Supply Agreement

    Noncircumvention

    Nonsolicitation

    CCIB Arbitration

    English language binding

    Invoicing conditions

PO Confirmation
Executed supply agreement
Accepted PO

Supplier(s) Prepayment Invoice
Pricing corresponds to PO
Terms correspond to PO

Prepayment Invoice to Client
Pricing corresponds to client PO
Terms correspond to client PO
Product ID

Progress Report
Mold fabrication schedule

Raw Material Data Sheet from Supplier
Conforms with client requirements and specs
Yellow Card compliant with regs

Raw Material Test Report
Conforms with client requirements and specs

Packaging and Container Design
Conforms with client requirements as per the purchase order

First Article Inspection Report
Raw material conforms with client specs
Critical dimensions
Universal dimensions
Conforms with regulations

Preproduction Sample Report
  Conforms with client requirements and specs
  Conforms with regulations

Midproduction Sample Report
  Conforms with client requirements and specs
  Conforms with regulations

Shipping Notice to Foreign Trade Company (FTC)
  Product name
  Product ID
  PO #
  Quantity
  # Skids
  Unit price
  Gross weight
  Net weight
  Volume
  Carton markings
  Remarks

Packaging and Loading Report
  Packages are dry
  Packages are stacked and loaded according to specification

Packing List from FTC
  Product name
  Product description
  Quantity
  Container # _____
  Seal # _____
  Quantities correspond to client PO

Onboard Bill of Lading
  Quantities correspond to client PO
  Delivery corresponds to client PO
  Container # _____
  Seal # _____

Supplier Invoice
  Were goods delivered on time / on spec?
  If not, special terms? _____
  Amount owed corresponds with PO terms
  Date due corresponds with PO terms
  Goods quantity references PO and packing list

Invoice to Client
  Carrier
  Master bill number
  Pricing corresponds to client PO

Proof of Delivery from Trucker via Shipper
  Product ID
  Product name
  Quantity

FTC Payment Instructions
  Supplier invoice #'s are correct
  Amounts correspond with amounts owed
  Special terms

Bank confirmation
  Amount corresponds with amount payable

Profitability and Performance Report
   Estimated costs versus actual costs
   Promised delivery date versus actual delivery date
   Defect rate
   Profit margin
   Learnings

This list is important, first, because it's a catalog of the documents you'll be dealing with. But it's also important for document quality control. Every document in a program references other documents. Make sure that the key elements in each document properly cross-reference.

For example, the invoice you received from your supplier should reference the same exact payment terms, quantities, and delivery date that your PO stated. Each time you get a project, shipping, or commercial document, you should compare the information in it with the ones you've already received to make sure there are no errors and that everything corresponds. These types of errors could be very costly.

WORKFLOW

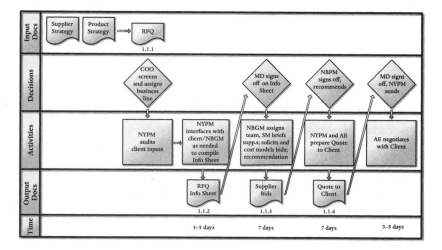

Managing Time

Time is a precious commodity in any import program and must be managed accordingly. I'm a big fan of project management software, which will help you track key documents, decisions, and your timeline. If you don't use software, you should still map out your project and timeline visually.

Notice how the flow chart on page 104 follows documents, decisions, activities, output documents, and time. You might even add an extra line here for cash.

You also need to monitor the project itself—how the engineering is going. Request project reports from your engineers at least on a weekly basis. Many China business veterans complain that they rarely see good inspection reports from their Chinese suppliers. An exemplary one appears on page 106. Note that the inspection report outlines each product item: its dimensions and tolerances, the inspection methodology used, and the results of the test. It's a good template to get you started.*

Step seven: Ship

It you want your goods to arrive on time, your documents must be filed properly. Fortunately, your freight forwarder is a document specialist. If you are unsure of what you are doing, your forwarder can fill out all forms for you (most likely, for a nominal fee), including the documents required by U.S. Customs, and any federal, state, and local agencies that might be regulating your commodity.

Your forwarder will then help you manage the flow of documents to make sure that nothing impedes your delivery. One holdup means the difference between an on-time delivery and tardiness. If your customer is a big retailer like Target or Wal-Mart, tardiness is a big no-no.

*For more document templates, visit AllTheT.com/templates.

Drawing No:	HHD-HCRF450LA	Revision:	C	Date Received BY QA: 05/02/06
Description:	Honda CRF-450 Shift Lever Arm			Quantity Received (By Q.A.): 1
Supplier:		Date: 05/02/06		Required: 1
P.O. Number		Inspected By: Xueqin,Tao		Date Inspected: 05/02/06

New Part	Resub-mission	Revision	New Tooling	Modified Tooling	Prototype	Sample	Initial Production	New Supplier	Fixtures	Special Request

Print Specifications				Sample number and results					
Item NO.	Dim.(Inch)	Plus Tol.	Minus Tol.	Inspect Method	1	2	3	4	5	Eng. Disp.
1	R.38	.01	.01	J	OK					
2	.130	.005	.005	B	.130-.134					
3	.455	.005	.005	B	.444-.446					E
4	.900	.005	.005	B	.859					E
5	.625	.005	.005	B	.625					
6	R.30	.01	.01	J	OK					
7	R.20X2	.01	.01	J	OK					
8	.263	.005	.005	B	.266					
9	.565	.005	.005	B	.563-.565					
10	.285	.005	.005	B	.281-.285					
11	M6x1			H	OK					
12	Φ.250/.520	.005	.005	B	Φ.245-.246/ .508-.511					E
13	3.253	.005	.005	B	3.232-3.234					E
14	R.40	.01	.01	J	N/A					
15	58°	30'	30'	G	58°					
16	31°	30'	30'	G	30.5°					
17	2.703	.005	.005	B	2.708-2.698					
18	.760	.005	.005	B	.742-.745					E
19	.590	.005	.005	B	.591					
20	R.50	.01	.01	J	OK					
21	R.10	.01	.01	J	OK					
22	Φ.325	.000	0.002	B	Φ.327-.328					
23	.607	.005	.005	B	0.602					
24	.360SLOT	.005	.005	B	.360-.361					
25	1.055	.005	.005	B	1.034-1.036					E
26	R.05	.01	.01	J	OK					

Engineering Dispositions: (Please Mark insert box ■ on all measurements out of specifications).
    A. Major Discrepancy-New Samples required.
    B. Minor Discrepancy-Must be corrected prior to production run-New Samples not required.
    C. Print Dimension or tolerance will be changed to conform to part.
    D. Print will not change-Deviation to accept parts for life of tool.
    E. Other (See comments below).

Comments:
    A-CMM,B-CALIPER,C-DEPTH CALIPER,D-HEIGHT CALIPER,E-MICROMETER(5~30MM),
    F-MICROMETER(50~600MM),G-GONIOMETER,H-THREAD GAUGE,I-TEMPLET,
    J-R GAUGE,K-GAUGE, L-SCLEROMETER,M-VISUAL

Remark:

For Evaluation use only
Rejected: ☐
Accepted: ☐
By: Date:

You get fined and ultimately kicked out of the supplier base for being late. So you want to make sure everything goes without a hitch in terms of document flow.

■

At least my partner and I can agree on something. We agree that the investment banker and the marketing guy need an industry specialist to help us solve our problems with defective goods and lateness. We reach out to the consultant who helped us perform our audit. She's been a good friend and adviser to the company since we began, and we enlist her support.

The first thing she does is define the basic metrics of our business. We need to be measuring three things at all times: the defect rate, the lateness rate, and the profitability. She will determine the relative success or failure of the team in supporting these three measures. She'll give the China staff six months to turn the operation around, after which she'll start firing people. (We'll go on to sack the entire China team and hire an entirely new group.)

She also begins personally interceding in supplier selection and project management. I am present at one of her negotiating sessions. She's a tough, quiet negotiator. That chain-smoking, hard-nosed factory manager is cowering in fear.

The term "dragon lady" comes to mind, and it's fitting, because it's a saying that's actually employed in Chinese parlance. Unlike in Japan, women in China have been able to rise through the ranks of government and industry and are rewarded for their toughness and smarts. We have such a dragon lady on our team, and she plays to the type.

But she's more than just tough. She's getting results. She hammers out a good price with the factory—a fair price, one that allows them a margin and us a margin. She's setting the project on a course for success.

She may be four foot nothing, but she's a giant in my book. Seeing her in action reminds me of that Fats Waller line, "There are four of us—me, your big feet, and you." I wish I had feet like hers. What a buyer.

Then something beautiful happens: we produce the goods up to spec, we deliver them on time, and we get paid. How sweet it is.

5

SELLING TO CHINA

The best revenge on a lousy customer
is to sell him more goods.

Our book of business surges again. Now we're facing a whole new vector of woes.

Like so many growing small businesses, we're illiquid when liquidity is our gasoline. To fund orders, we're going out of pocket to pay for raw materials and production but aren't recouping our money until much later in the cycle. We're lurching from one order to the next, while I'm running down to Miami every other week to shake the tin cup among an investor group that is growing weary of our appeals for help. Equity financing is keeping corporate body and soul together as we grow, but we won't be able to sustain that for long.

Blessedly, we're finding new ways to make money, and that helps. We start to see the big picture: how trade flows are circular. Even the likes of us, a small contract manufacturer and importer, can conduct two-way trade like a multinational corporation.

Every product has an input, and many inputs come from the United States. In this case, it's plastics. We're tasked with making lids for industrial storage tanks. But not just any lids—the tanks must house toxic chemicals, so the lids must seal tightly. They're made with polypropylene, and we discover excellent sources for reground PP in the United States. It's cheaper than the virgin material, and its quality lives up to the product specifications. We identify a U.S. supplier, buy the resin, put it in a container, and ship it to China, where it is injection-molded into the various parts that go into the application, assembled, packed, and exported back to the States.

Many shipping containers sail to China empty. So freight rates from the United States to the mainland are usually much cheaper than going the other way. This gives you some flexibility to be creative. Even importers can be exporters. A great many U.S. businesses, in fact, export raw materials or unfinished goods for fabrication in China, only to reimport the finished goods once they are completed.

Some of these firms are called "tolling businesses." They export raw materials to a special economic zone in China, usually near the port, where the materials are processed before being reexported back to the States. The goods receive special tax and duty treatment.[1]

Although we're not tolling, we discover that by moving upstream and participating in the export of raw materials, we can not only save our clients more money (and secure a little more profit margin for ourselves) but better control the inputs to the products, and thereby more closely safeguard their quality.

Now if we could only get those darned sealants to work on the lids, we'd be in business. I suppose NASA isn't the only manufacturer that produces leaky O rings.

MEET CHINA, THE IMPORTER

While working on the polypropylene lids deal, my gumshoeing on China's import market for recycled plastic reveals a surprising fact. The market in China for U.S. recycled resins is growing at over 30 percent a year. I'm floored. With a little more investigation, I find out that China is, far and away, the fastest-growing market for U.S. products and services, in general. U.S. sales to China have grown five times faster than to any other market in the world.

I'm scratching my head. All I see in the news are stories about our widening trade and account deficits with China—and nothing about this export bonanza. Nothing about the opportunity for American firms to build vast new markets for their goods and services. Just diatribes blaming China for a host of economic woes.

Well, if you're angry, consider this. As the old cloak-and-suiters used to say: *The best revenge on a lousy customer is to sell him more goods!* If you're sore at China, and you think the Chinese are getting the better of you in the global economy, get in there and sell them more stuff.

China's buying. In fact, China buys more from the world than it sells. China is the world's number-one importer of many commodities, such as steel, aluminum, copper, tin, iron ore, and cement.[2] China is the second-largest importer of oil, behind the United States.

In 2003, Chinese consumers bought 33 percent of the world's air conditioners, 18 percent of the world's televisions, 15 percent of the world's DVD players, 14 percent of the world's refrigerators, and 13 percent of the world's mobile phones.[3] China is the third-largest car market in the world, and it's on track to be the number-one market within the decade.

As its demand for American raw materials and agricultural products soars, some have complained that China has relegated advanced economies like the United States to "third world" status. True, China buys American cotton and soybeans, pulp and plastic, iron ore and steel, and other raw materials in vast quantities.

But China is also increasingly buying engineered goods from the United States. Because it lacks the capability to make these products on its own, China must import most of the sophisticated or "value-added" components that go into a final product—from specialty chemicals to auto parts to microchips.

That's why American exports to China are booming in so many product categories. From 2003 to 2004, China's imports of American specialty chemicals grew by 48 percent; electrical machinery and equipment, by 36 percent; optical and medical equipment, by 59 percent; power generation equipment, by 28 percent; and so on. These are staggering figures, and ones you don't hear about in the media or on the political stump.

So even though China is—slowly—learning how to make goods that are more sophisticated than clothes, toys, and housewares, America is quickly climbing the value chain in what it can *export* to China. The United States is increasingly becoming a top source for many of the goods and services that the Chinese consume: premium foods, modern conveniences, modern pharmaceuticals and medical care, modern technology, and modern services. China's various market needs play right into the sweet spot of American industry.

But markets in China cannot simply be switched on like a spigot. Markets must be assiduously built. In many cases, the Chinese may not even know they *need* you yet, such as in the case of insurance. Or, your product or service may not exist. Dairy Queen found that lesson out the hard way, when they sought to enter the Chinese markets, only to discover no one knew what a dessert treat was.[4]

Solution? Teach them. Show them how terrific your product is. And if it doesn't jibe with local tastes, then adapt. Dairy Queen went on to modify its menu to suit local tastes and today is a thriving brand in China.

Consumers must often be educated about your product, and that demands an investment of time, dollars, and intestinal fortitude. Yet many American companies of all sizes—in both goods and services— are succeeding. They're building an installed customer base in China.

And that's akin to hitching your wagon to a star. Because the Chinese people have more disposable income today than at any time in modern history. Per capita income grew more than sixfold from 1980 to 2003, and wages have tripled over the past few years—a trajectory of growth that has swelled the ranks of the middle class at a rate not seen since the industrialization of the United States, Western Europe, and Japan.

The World Bank estimates that 130 million Chinese earn enough to be considered middle class. A hundred and thirty million people! That's larger than the entire population of Japan. Or the combined populations of France and England. And China is just getting started.

Who is this voracious urban consumer? The profile will seem familiar to Americans. China today is much more Calvinist than Communist, much more Monaco than Mao. Nowadays, the moneyed are considered the elect in China, not the Party. Your status is connected with how rich you look. I once asked a Chinese marketing manager of a multinational cosmetics company what he saw as most important in doing business on the mainland. "Image," he said. "The right suit, the right haircut, the Louis Vuitton luggage."

Louis Vuitton luggage? Believe it or not, Chinese professionals save for months to pay for these luxury goods. And intead of Mao suits, Chinese men prefer dark, Italian-cut ones, often leaving the large, square brand labels sewn onto their sleeves (labels that we, in the West, snip off). They will assert the sleeve conspicuously, as if they were the bearer of a four-carat engagement ring that they want to casually draw your attention to.

Clearly, what's considered stylish in the West, then, isn't always a direct corollary in China. Recently, tony Shanghai residents took to sporting their pajamas as formal evening wear. While strolling on the Bund in jacket and tie, I was sneered at contemptuously by a couple clad in just their jammies. I might as well have shown up to a fancy dress ball in grimy sweatpants. There was nothing unusual or sumptuous about their nightwear, by the way. No Robert Montgomery pocket square, stuffed rakishly into the pajama pocket; no Mae West muumuu, a long frilly boa to match. Just simple top-and-bottom sets. But they deported themselves as if they were the height of sophistication. The implicit cultural message here is Calvinist: we're rich enough to afford pajamas. Aren't we the cat's pajamas?

While Mao himself may have scorned this turn from Dialectical Materialism to just plain materialism, Deng probably would have approved. "To get rich is glorious," he once said. Indeed, the shift marks a radical departure from the old. Simply apprehending the concept of brands and fashion is a leap of cultural cognition that many emerging markets have yet to make. And American brands loom large on China's cultural landscape. You see them everywhere.

BARRIERS TO ENTRY

Some of them got lucky, like Buick. Brand equity was thrust upon them. The old Communist Party apparatchiks used to drive big Buicks. So Buick became associated with power and prestige. It's no big surprise then that today, Buick is a top-selling car in China, and one with a completely different brand profile than in the States. Over here, Buick is struggling to appeal to a demographic beyond pensioners. In China, Buick is considered sexy and opulent. You see them mostly in jet black—sleek, cocky versions of their apologetic American counterparts.

Unfortunately, however, most U.S. companies in China have not had Buick's luck. Even the most recognizable American icons have had to build markets for their products and services. The good news, though, is that American brands have prestige in China. The United States is esteemed for superior know-how and technology. Your country of origin is an edge in building your brand.

In addition to educating your consumers, you've also got to contend with some obstacles to successful sales: namely, China's complex regulatory environment, bad credit support, and fragmented distribution networks. Regulatory compliance in each province varies, but on average, you've got to follow twelve regulatory steps to launch a business, which takes an average of forty-one days, if you know what you're doing. (If you don't know what you're doing, it can take years.) Other regulations govern contract enforcement, hiring and firing workers, registering property, and closing a business. These regulations often vary by municipality. Western law firms with established offices in China should be able to help you navigate these complexities.

You'll also be delighted to hear that credit information sharing and the legal rights of borrowers and lenders are among the worst in Asia. The International Finance Corporation (IFC) gave China a score of two out of a possible ten (compared to the regional average of five) for the "coverage, scope, quality and accessibility of credit information available" in China and how well "collateral and bankruptcy laws facilitate lending." That means it's hard to know whether or not your Chinese customers are creditworthy, and you have little recourse if they default. Don't rely on databases and published reports. Your eyes and ears are the best guides to whether your clients are solvent. Visit them.

Another major obstacle to successful sales is the lack of national distribution networks. Getting product to customers is challenging for both foreign and domestic firms alike. The larger Chinese retailers and consumer product companies, like Huawei Electronics, TCL, and Lenovo, have patched together networks comprising thousands of local outlets to overcome this problem. But most Chinese firms struggle with distribution, fighting local protectionism and regulations, just as foreign entrants do.

Despite the barriers, though, firms are flourishing. B&Q, the do-it-yourself retailer, is a case in point. In Britain, their 300 stores are served by 600 suppliers. Their 48 Chinese stores, however, are served by 1,800 suppliers. Chinese regulations make it costly and complex to do business, yet B&Q continues to grow.

More and more Western firms like B&Q are blazing a trail into China's markets and proving that it's possible to succeed despite the complex operating environment. That's good, because in both products and services, there are so many exciting markets to enter.

WHICH MARKETS?

The economies of the United States and China are largely complementary. What we do well, China tends to need. But just because something sells well here, don't presume it'll sell well there, as flatworlders suggest. Rather, analyze markets and consumer demand from the bottom up and the top down.

From the bottom up, focus like a laser on customer need. Is anyone in China using your product or service today? If so, who sells it? If not, why not? Is this a need that is not currently being fulfilled? Often, you've got to introduce your product to the market and educate customers on how to use it. But sometimes a dire need will be unmet in the marketplace, such as the need for mining safety equipment or environmental services or water treatment products. Measure the need first, and the barriers to addressing that need, before you do anything else.

Since you won't find any accurate market research, though, the best way to learn is by applying the Warren Buffet technique. He relies on the smell of his own nose. He visits. He tastes. He samples. He makes up his own mind. In considering sales opportunities in China, you should do the same. Go. Look at behaviors and buying patterns. Look at how other brands are marketing themselves. Visit your target cities. How big are they? What is the approximate size of your target customer group? What are the obstacles to entry and scaling the business?

From the top down, you can look at trends. Export opportunities arise from the congruencies of the two economies. If China's flooding us with toys and housewares, it's good to be in the recycled plastic business. If they're flooding us with office furniture, it's good to be in the lumber business. If they're flooding us with steel I-bars, it's good to be in the iron ore business.

But more than products, services have areas of congruence, too. As China's industrial and consumer sectors boom, they need legal, banking, insurance, consulting, advertising, architecture, and a host of other services which America can provide, and which China, largely, cannot.

The services sector, in fact, is one of China's big blind spots. Last year, China went so far as to revalue its GDP by an additional 17 percent, attributable mostly to services. Oops. We forgot about a whole sector of our economy. We'll just tack on another 17 percent to last year's output.

In part, this is because China just doesn't get it yet. A formerly Marxist economy, they're still figuring out how valuable services are to an economy. But another reason for this sudden uptick is because the service industries in China are dominated by private firms, which usually underreport their contribution to the GDP in an effort to avoid scrutiny and higher taxes. The authorities are getting wise to them. So the numbers are starting to reflect more of what's actually happening on the ground.

Today, services are now estimated to make up 41 percent of China's GDP.[5] That's still low, compared with other developed economies. And as China's industries and middle class grow, the demand for services will keep rising. Let's take a quick look at three service industries: insurance, advertising, and law.

For the insurance industry, China is a potential gold mine. Less than 4 percent of China's population have insurance[6]—a number that is sure to grow. Until now, the market has been dominated by the central government, but foreign competition is growing as WTO requirements are met.

There were approximately thirty-one insurance companies in China in 2000: fourteen domestic insurers and seventeen foreign insurers. By the end of 2005, there were eighty-three insurers in China. Forty-one were foreign firms. Market access is opening, and conditions are becoming more favorable for insurance companies.

But even though the restrictions that govern setting up shop in China are loosening, there are still some you'll need to be aware of. For example, in order to qualify for a business license, a foreign insurer must have a rep office in China for a minimum of two years, have a parent company with $5 billion in assets, have thirty continuous years of underwriting, and be from a country with a sound financial regulatory system.[7]

Insurance is an infant industry in China, and both companies and consumers are unsure what to expect and what to demand. What's more, insurance companies have difficulty predicting risk, thus making pricing difficult. China lacks actuarial standards—though there is a joint project between Deloitte & Touche and the University of Connecticut to help further develop this field.[8] Yet, despite the challenges to market penetration, the insurance industry presents a tremendous opportunity for Western firms.

Advertising agencies face a similar situation: a vast, wide-open market with some barriers to entry to be cognizant of. There are already about 89,552 advertising agencies in China, including more than 385 foreign joint ventures.[9] As you'd expect, most of the big Western agencies are already in China, through staffed branch offices that often subcontract production work to local vendors.

Despite all the players in the field, though, the market is still growing. The Standards Group, for example, is an ad agency that was started in 2002 by foreign nationals in China—without forming a U.S. operation first. This small but growing agency has no trouble winning new business. They receive about two inbound inquiries a week, and feel the market is still huge and relatively untapped for advertising services. As China's companies try to elbow their way through the brutal competition, they increasingly see advertising, promotion, and marketing as key ingredients to acquiring and retaining customers and differentiating themselves in the crowded marketplace.

Though winning new business has not been a problem, acclimating clients to agency services has. Chinese companies are usually unaccustomed to working with an ad agency and often burn up the agency time and resources on fool's errands. "Managing client expectations" is the advertising account exec's mantra in the United States. In China, though, you need to build client expectations from scratch before you can manage them. The Standards Group reports some success in this area; over time, both they and their clients are learning how to communicate better. And Chinese companies are coming to understand the different aspects of an integrated communications program.

While ad agencies must educate their clients on the value of their services, law firms must adapt their services so they are valued by their clients. Though China faces a severe lack of lawyers, foreign law firms can do just about everything in China—except practice law and invoice for their services. They're not allowed to set up their own operating business that can issue invoices and collect payments, but instead are permitted only to set up a representative office. The head of the office must be a partner, must live in China, and must have practiced in his or her home country for at least three years. And what's more, law firms must certify that all attorneys at the firm have no ethical or criminal violations on their records. The same standards do not apply to other industries.

If foreign lawyers are not allowed to actually practice law in China—not allowed to appear in the court, not allowed to render an official opinion on Chinese law—then how do law firms add value?

They've become local fixers. In addition to advising their clients on which corporate form they should take and how to navigate the Chinese legal bureaucracy, they also work the softer side of market entry: connecting their clients with the necessary business and government contacts in China.

For example, a friend of mine was interested in starting a nightclub in Shanghai. This type of business falls in a very gray area of Chinese law. I found out in trying to help him that, yes, it's important to have all your paperwork and contracts in order, but more important is the need for cover from the local police department and government. If the police were okay with the nightclub operations, he'd stay open. In this case, a good law firm would not only draft up the contracts but would also cement the relationships with the necessary people at the police department and the municipal government.

You can work China's complex system and succeed. And many American firms today are doing just that. But before approaching the markets, remember to check whether your product or service is restricted under the arms embargo—that it is not deemed "dual use," affording the Chinese an opportunity to improve their military capability. Seemingly common products are sometimes construed as "dual use": for example, a company that wanted to export a special air bag technology to China was stopped from doing so. The air bag was deployed using a munition that could be construed as weaponry. Check with your local U.S. Commerce office to make sure you comply.

Outside of munitions and weapons technology, just about every other market is open for business. Here are a few especially tantalizing ones.

Agriculture

Agriculture presents a huge market opportunity for both large businesses and small. Today, agricultural, fishery, and forestry exports to China are at an all-time high, estimated at $8.1 billion in 2004.[10] China's demand for ag products, as the fourth-largest importer of agricultural goods in the world, is expected to keep rising.[11]

Here are a few specific market segments to consider:

Wine and Beer

People in southern China are drinking more beer and wine these days because their incomes have doubled within just the past few years. (As good a reason as any to celebrate.) Imports still represent a small portion of the market, though. Tsingtao is an old successful joint venture that makes and distributes lager in China, but there's room for more imported brands. You'll need to educate your customer base as to the differences in quality and flavors—not an impossible task, and one that presents a lot of upside.

Livestock and Livestock Products

U.S. pork exports to China in 2004 shot up over 100 percent, and continued strong growth is forecast. Cattle exports rose 232 percent between 2005 and 2006, a reflection of strong demand in dairy. However, China still restricts the import of other bovine products, such as live cattle, beef products, and nonprotein tallow, because of mad cow disease. Specifically, bovine semen and embryos will start to be traded, via a new import protocol signed in 2004, but Chinese officials have requested that they inspect the U.S. embryo and semen collection facilities first. (That's a dog and pony show I would rather not see.)

Poultry and Poultry Products

After banning poultry imports when a case of avian flu broke out in Delaware in 2004, China has opened its markets again. China's inspection standards are tougher today on poultry products. They're also cracking down on smuggling from Hong Kong, which has been widespread in the past. Most container traffic will now head directly to the mainland.

Fish Meal

China's fish meal production is declining. They can thank shrinking fish stocks. But demand is still high, pushing prices up. China's estimated consumption in 2004 was 386,000 metric tons. According to USDA figures, China imports about 1 to 1.3 million metric tons per annum.

Fresh Deciduous Fruit

China is the world's largest producer (and consumer) of apples, pears, and grapes, making up 50 percent of world apple production,

65 percent of world pear production, and 40 percent of world table grape production, according to the USDA. It's not enough. Imports of many fruits are going up, as China volumes are decreasing. Fruit entry requirements that were recently issued might have an impact on trade of all deciduous fruit, especially re-exports from Hong Kong to China, so do your research before attempting to enter this market.

Food Processing Ingredients

With more money in their pockets, Chinese consumers are demanding higher-quality processed food. This industry is growing fast in China.

■

If you intend to export or sell agricultural products into China, not only should you contact the U.S. Department of Commerce, but you should also be aware that each product segment has its own trade representative in China that can help you. They include: the California Prune Board, the Raisin Administrative Committee, the U.S. Dry Pea and Lentil Council, and Cotton Council International. Each industry group in China will be a good source for information and market-specific assistance. (I'm trying to stand up the Pastrami Commissariat. Any joiners?)

It's also a good idea to contact the Department of Agriculture, which runs many offices in-country to help keep markets open and hospitable. They'll help you get your bearings, too.

Agrochemicals

The United States has been the top exporter of pesticides to China for several years. China is trying to regulate the market to prevent toxic runoff, so low-toxicity pesticides from the United States have favorable market prospects in China. (Though you may, as a foreign entrant, have to comply with some tough product-testing criteria.)

In terms of fertilizer, China's WTO commitments spell good news for exporters. In a market that has been controlled by a state-owned monopoly, foreign firms will now gain the right to bring fertilizers into China and distribute them. There are still some quotas to be aware of, though. Import volumes inside the quota are levied a duty of 4 percent, while imports that exceed the quota are levied a duty of 50 percent.

Air Traffic Management Equipment

China is the world's fastest-growing export market for U.S. air traffic management (ATM) equipment. China spent $1 billion on ATM improvements over the last ten years, and it is forecast to spend an additional $1.2 billion in the next ten years. The bulk of this machinery will be imported—local sources cannot deliver U.S. quality yet.

As you can imagine, China's air traffic is growing. Volume has increased between 8 and 10 percent per annum and is expected to grow 10 to 15 percent a year over the next ten years. Right now, airports along the Beijing-Guangzhou corridor account for 76 percent of domestic flights, but more volume is expected in central and western China.

China's civil aviation administration is working in close cooperation with the U.S. Federal Aviation Administration (FAA) on designing and implementing China's air traffic control system. So, there will be a pronounced demand for U.S. ATM equipment. China is investing the necessary funds to build a safe, reliable system and is looking to the FAA to ensure safety during the upcoming Olympic Games in 2008.

Here are some especially good opportunities for U.S. companies: upgrading control centers in eastern and central China; improving ground-to-air communication facilities as well as automatic dependent surveillance of routes in western China to increase control and capacity in this region; and deploying VHF communication, navigation, and secondary surveillance radar systems.

Automotive Components

China's WTO accession is a boon to U.S. automakers. Tariffs on automobiles and auto parts have been reduced substantially, and U.S. auto companies now are permitted to distribute most of their products in any part of China.

As a general rule, Chinese auto firms do not stack up well against their American competitors. Lacking capital, their operations are usually small, with little to no research-and-development capability. Therefore, U.S. goods, considered higher in quality, are in demand, and many U.S. firms are already selling their automobile parts to the Chinese markets. China is encouraging the investment in and development of local automotive capability, but this will take many years.

Notice how the launch of Chinese cars that can be exported to the U.S. has been postponed again and again. Now Chery and the other Chinese auto market leaders are talking about postponing another five to ten years. They'll need it. The disparity between Western and Chinese automotive capability is great, and it can only be redressed through many years of investment, training, and capacity building.

In the meantime, China presents the single largest market opportunity Detroit has ever seen. There's already quite a large enterprise base to sell components into. China today, according to the China Association of Automobile Manufacturers, has 6,224 automotive enterprises: motor vehicle manufacturing (145), vehicle refitting (536), motorcycle production (1,162), auto engine production (58), and auto parts manufacturing (4,323). These Chinese firms are importing goods from the United States in tremendous volumes.

Shanghai is the center of component manufacturing. Shanghai General Motors, Delphi (the profitable division that's not filing for bankruptcy), Visteon, and other big American firms are already here. Shanghai is a good place to start if you're thinking auto.

China's Automotive Components
Market Information (USD Millions)

	2003	2004	2005 *(projected)*
Total market size	22,600	28,800	35,800
Total local production	8,000	9,200	10,580
Total exports	3,220	4,500	6,300
Total imports	5,940	6,500	6,800
Imports from the U.S.	510	585	620

1. Statistics collected from National Bureau of Statistics and *World Trade Atlas*.
2. 2005 figures are projected based on 2005, 3rd quarter data.
3. Automotive component figures based on five categories: engine parts, chassis parts, automotive body, electrical systems, and general parts.

Source: U.S. Commerce Department

Especially good market opportunities include: auto accessories; fuel cell technology; key auto parts and components such as drive axle assembly, air suspension frame, automatic electric servo steering system, transmission box, compound meter, etc.; electronic devices and instruments (control systems, global positioning systems); engines for cars, trucks, and motorcycles; and casting blanks.

Coal Mining Equipment

China remains a coal-burning economy. Coal accounts for about two-thirds of its total primary energy consumption. China must continue to invest in coal production to keep pace with the country's energy demands, and experts believe China must invest at least $151 billion in coal infrastructure by 2020.

But when it comes to heavy coal mining machines and equipment, U.S. firms have a competitive advantage. China is manufacturing a wide array of machines, but its technologies are ten to fifteen years behind the United States in terms of quality, environmental protection, safety, and efficiency. So even though the market is dominated by local firms, U.S. companies face good long-term prospects.

In addition to production, safety is a dire problem in Chinese coal mines. In an eerie transpacific echo, mining accidents were happening in 2005 at an alarming rate in both the United States and China. To some degree, small, unsafe mines were to blame in both cases. Accidents killed over 6,000 Chinese miners in 2005.[12] The government is taking action and is suing to shut down 4,000 small operators.

Only 35 percent of China's more than 25,000 mines have proper safety equipment. China intends to invest over $6 billion in the coming years on safety equipment. This is a big opportunity for small and mid-sized U.S. firms. Best prospects include: coal mining safety equipment, security equipment, gas control systems, and fire monitoring and control equipment.

Construction Equipment

The market for equipment has boomed in tandem with China's real estate market. American firms like Caterpillar, John Deere, and Terex have already established themselves here and have risen with the tide. However, China's efforts to cool its overheating real estate market will probably put a damper on construction equipment sales. Also, American firms will face tough competition from local firms, as well as from Japanese, Korean, and European manufacturers.

The best opportunities for U.S. exports of construction equipment include: self-propelled bulldozers, angle dozers, graders, levelers, scrapers, mechanical shovels, excavators shovel loaders, tramping machines, and road rollers.

Banking Technology

The WTO has pried open China's banking sector to U.S. firms. In the agreement, China must allow foreign-controlled banks full competitive access to its banking markets by December 11, 2006. In anticipation of the increased competition, Chinese banks have already begun to modernize their technologies and back-office systems, which are primitive. They've got a lot of catching up to do.

Chinese banks spent almost $3 billion in 2005 on IT products. Investment is expected to continue to rise sharply. Chinese banks are tough customers, and they prefer dependable, practical products with strong after-sales support.

Banks spent the largest percentage of their IT outlay (16.4 percent) on applications software in 2005. In 2006, they've purchasing server and network hardware. The best export opportunities in the years to come for American IT companies selling systems and equipment to the financial sector include: credit cards, online banking products, hardware, IT services, network security, disaster recovery systems, risk management systems, core banking systems, payment systems, and anti-money-laundering systems.

Credit Cards

China's credit card market is booming. By the end of 2004 alone, 762 million bank cards were issued; 664 million were debit cards, and 98 million were credit cards, according to People's Bank of China. Lots of banks issue credit cards today—over 150, including China's Big Four banks, as well as a number of second-tier city banks. The state-owned commercial banks also issue dual-currency cards, so Chinese can buy goods in dollars overseas *and* yuan when at home.

Credit card usage in the coastal cities is high. About 20 percent of all purchases in Beijing, Shanghai, Guangzhou, and Shenzhen are made with bank cards. (The national average is about 5 percent.) China has set up a national switch center and has built bank card network service centers in eighteen cities. At the end of 2005, China had approximately 500,000 POS machines and 70,000 ATMs. About 300,000 merchants in China accept banking cards.

Opportunities for U.S. firms in the credit market include:

credit-card-related hardware; credit-card-related software for banks and merchants; call-center-related products; and credit, risk, and client management software and training for banks.

Education and Training

Education is a critical component of China's continued growth, and the Chinese know it. Chinese consumers said they would spend as much as a tenth of their savings on education—putting the market at about $80 billion, according to the U.S. Commerce Department! China is boosting its investment in education from 2.5 percent of GDP to 4 percent (up from $50 billion in 2004).

The market is large. In 2005, there were 23 million Chinese students attending 1,552 colleges and universities. And more and more Chinese are enrolling in programs online for vocational, certificate, and career training. U.S. universities are already very active in China's education market. They currently lead the market in joint venture MBA programs.

China is bullish on e-learning. Its Ministry of Education is funding a project that will wire all of China's 550,871 K-12 schools with e-learning systems by 2010. It's also promoting e-learning among China's universities. Many private companies have begun to service this sector (offering certification exam prep and vocational training online, for example), but there is a lot of opportunity for U.S. firms to build and hold market share. Opportunities include MBA certificate programs; vocational training; and language instruction, among many others.

Environmental Products and Services

This is a tremendous market for U.S. firms. China is racing to meet its own curbs on pollution, lest the country drown in health-care costs incurred in treating its poisoned populace. In the next five years, Beijing alone will spend almost $7 billion on environmental projects, according to the U.S. Commerce Department. On environmental protection, $800 million will be invested in preventing coal burning pollution. Natural gas storage tanks and pipelines are also being built; the use of clean natural gas and liquid natural gas (such as in buses and taxis) is growing; European Standard II automobile emission standards are being implemented; and waste dumping and preprocessing capabilities are being upgraded.

That's just Beijing. Every major city is investing billions of dollars in environmental products and services. In fact, "green" is a gold rush in China. Environmentally friendly raw materials, building materials, automotive supplies, and energy supplies are all now very much in demand in China.

Franchising

KFC has 2,100 franchises in China alone. McDonald's has over 700. Retailing and catering have led the way, but today, new forms of franchises are opening up, including business services, family services, automotive care, and so on.

A weak regulatory environment plagues franchisers today. Add to that a paucity of qualified franchisees and some thorny recent legislation that requires you to operate two company-owned stores in China for one year before franchising can begin—and you can see that there are some barriers to entry to consider. Still, opportunities exist in executive search, dry cleaning, real estate, training, and car rental and repair services.

Safety and Security

By 2020, this market is estimated to hit $30 billion. (The market was $7 billion in 2003.) A lot of China's investment is pouring into airport security. China is building 108 new airports through 2011, and security is of paramount concern. Fire protection equipment, X-ray scanners, metal detectors, portable detectors, and other equipment are needed.

Here are some other growth opportunities: entrance guard communication systems, inspection control systems, detection equipment, warning systems, and fire protection equipment.

Semiconductor Industry

China is not only the world's third-largest market for semiconductors after Japan and America, it's also the fastest-growing. Chinese official statistics estimated the market size at $35 billion in 2004. All sectors of the semi industry are growing.

But because of lagging manufacturing capability, China must still depend on imports for the majority of its integrated circuits, integrated circuits testing and assembly equipment, packaging equipment, and design and development tools.

Major Semiconductor Projects
under Construction or Planned in China

Company	Total investment (Million USD)	Wafer size	Location
Hejian Technology	1500	12"	Suzhou
Hynix	2000	12"	Wuxi
Sim-BCD	660	8"	Shanghai
TSMC	1120	8"	Shanghai
Prima	100	8"	Changzhou
Belling	340	8"	Shanghai
Kexi	300	8"	Shenyang
Nanke	186	8"	Guangzhou

Source: China Semiconductor Industry Association (CSIA), Nov. 2004

Machinery

As China's manufacturers take on the best of the world's foreign competition, they're ramping up their consumption of advanced machines and equipment. This represents a giant market opportunity for the machine tool industry—especially in Detroit. In fact, it is the auto industry that is driving China's thirst for machine tools, representing over half of China's machine tool industry.

In terms of specific tools, U.S. exports to China in 2005 of metal cutting machine tools rose 20.6 percent ($2 billion), and exports of metal forming machine tools rose 40.26 percent ($1 billion). Opportunities include: grinders, lathes, spindles, tool carriages, ball-screws, tool system manipulators, high-speed protectors, and precision tools.

Marine Industries

The best prospects in China's marine industries include shipbuilding, pleasure boats, and port-related accessories and sea transportation.

Shipbuilding

Based on current growth rates, by 2015 China will be the top shipbuilder in the world. But China needs technology, equipment, and management.[13] The best prospects for shipbuilding are cutting and welding technology and related equipment, raw materials, coating equipment and coating materials, technology for ship design and construction, equipment maintenance, GPS navigation, and onboard computer systems.

Recreational Boats

Chinese are spending more money on recreational boating, and the market is estimated to reach $10 billion over the coming decade. Local government, real estate developers, and boat builders are all investing in this industry. Opportunities for U.S. companies include pleasure boats, accessories, and marina planning and construction.

Port and Sea Transportation

China is already the world's number-one location for port throughput, and volume is still going up rapidly. China is investing heavily in port and waterway infrastructure to accommodate the increasing flow of goods. Eight ports (Shanghai, Shenzhen, Qingdao, Tianjin, Guangzhou, Xiamen, Ningbo, and Dalian) rank in the world's top fifty in terms of container traffic.

Most ports are increasing capacity and continuing to modernize. Products and technologies in high demand include vessel traffic management information systems, laser-docking systems, terminal tractors, dredging equipment, and security equipment for International Ship and Port Security Codes (ISPS).

Liquefied Natural Gas Industry

China has historically supplied all of its own natural gas, but its demand is outstripping its supply. China will need to spend about $27 billion to build natural gas and liquefied natural gas (LNG) infrastructure. This represents a big market opportunity for U.S. manufacturers and suppliers of LNG equipment, including gas power stations, LNG carriers, and equipment for infrastructure and transportation.

China will require tanks, gas-fueled power plants, receiving terminals, cycle gas turbines, and gas pipelines to transport LNG after gasification.

Power Generation

To keep up with its energy demands, China plans to spend nearly *$2 trillion* on upgrading its power generation, transmission, and distribution over the next thirty years. As part of this plan, the government is encouraging the development of alternative and renewable fuel sources with big incentives and tax breaks.

The most competitive products and services for U.S. companies will be in alternative power supplies (including wind, solar, and nuclear); advanced thermal power generation (including large-capacity gas turbines, large-capacity coal-fired power generation equipment, clean coal technology, and combine cycle technology); power dispatching systems; and ultra-high-voltage transmission equipment and management systems. Safety equipment also has strong market potential for U.S. firms.

Software

The software industry in China is finally picking up. After a decade of stagnant growth, 2005 saw a 17 percent jump in sales of software in China. The elimination in 2003 of tariffs on software imports probably has something to do with the sudden growth spurt. But given that the industry is being helped along by the government (rebates and incentive programs), it is expected that the software industry will continue to grow in China.

Foreign firms hold about 65 percent of China's total software market, though competition is fierce. Many opportunities for software vendors will open up with the government's new plan to develop the IT infrastructure across all industries: finance, telecommunications, banking, education, medical, construction, media, communication, and manufacturing.

Telecommunications

By 2010, the number of telephone users in China is predicted to hit one billion—and Internet users to hit 200 million! Telephone service is expected to be available in every single Chinese village by the end of 2010. China's vast telecom sector is going through big changes, and that spells big market opportunities for U.S. firms.

Mobile Communications

China's two major mobile carriers (China Unicom and China Mobile) are expanding their networks and will continue to have need for base stations and switches. But as 3G licenses are issued for third-generation wireless technology, there is talk of a market restructuring and the admission of new players. The 3G market has good potential for U.S. firms that sell telecom hardware and services.

Value-Added Services

As the telecom market in China becomes more competitive for fixed line and mobile, operators are increasingly positioning themselves as value-added service providers. This strategy allows them to grow more revenue streams and defend market share. Chinese carriers are therefore avidly looking for new applications or utilities that might differentiate them in the marketplace.

Online Gaming/Mobile Gaming

Content for games seems to be a good market for foreign firms that can customize their offerings and provide local service. Game developers should seek to work directly with Chinese telecom operators or with ISPs.

Water and Wastewater Treatment

China is in the middle of a dire water crisis. Among the 669 cities in China, nearly 400 suffer from inadequate water supply, among which 110 cities, including Beijing, Shanghai, and Dalian, suffer from severe water shortage. China's water table is sinking a meter a year in some areas in north China, and its potable water supply is only one-quarter of the total. Add to that the factor of water pollution and weak infrastructure, and you begin to see the magnitude of the problem.

Water infrastructure was until recently a state monopoly. China has recently reformed its water and treatment industry, creating many opportunities for foreign firms: biological denitrification and phosphorus removal technologies; membrane separation and manufacturing technologies and equipment; manufacturing technology of anaerobic biological reactors; high-concentration organic wastewater treatment technology and equipment; series-standard water and wastewater treatment equipment with high efficiency; water-saving technologies and equipment; water treatment agents; monitoring instruments; and natural water body rehabilitation technology.

Medical Equipment

China is a big market for medical equipment—right now it's ranked the world's eighth. But it continues to grow fast, as China rushes to modernize and scale its ramshackle health care system. China's top three suppliers of medical equipment in 2004 were the United States, in the lead at $904 million worth of goods, Japan, and Germany. Sales, especially of high-technology medical systems, have been growing 20 percent per year.

Chinese doctors and hospitals see U.S. products as superior in technology and quality. And despite barriers to entry with regard to pricing and testing, this market presents good long-term growth opportunities for U.S. firms.

■

That's a dizzying array of markets. And guess what? I only scratched the surface. There are a great many more markets in China for U.S. goods and services. Where to begin?

Well, if you haven't investigated how the U.S. government can help you, I strongly urge you to do so. Point your Web browser to the relevant office at the International Trade Administration—a division of the U.S. Department of Commerce. The division is made up of four offices, each of which you may find helpful to your import and export needs. Especially valuable is the Gold Key program offered by the Foreign Commercial Service. Tailored to exporters that have more than one export program under their belt, the service provides on-the-ground market research and ten real business leads.

Once you've reached out for help if you need it, and determined what market you're going to target, you'll need to consider how to best sell your product.

SHOULD I USE AN AGENT OR A DISTRIBUTOR?

The advantage of working with Chinese agents or distributors is that they will most likely be familiar with local conditions. Before WTO accession, foreign companies were not allowed to distribute goods inside China. On paper, they're allowed to today, but the rules are murky and still under contention.

The main drawback to working with an agent or distributor, however, is that you will have difficulty achieving a unique position in the marketplace. Your goods will usually be presented alongside others—probably in the same category.

Even if you are in a commodity market, this should cause concern. A small firm that sells limestone was determined not to be relegated to this pack. They understood that if they were perceived in the marketplace as a commodity (even though their product *was* a commodity), they'd be in a race to the bottom on pricing. Today, they are exporting limestone to China, and selling it at four times the price asked by local Chinese quarries.

One way they achieved this feat was by opting against the distributor/agent route. They went to China and visited the large trade fair for the stone industry. They scoped out the scene and met some people. They looked at the competition. To their dismay, they learned that their product, delivered, was priced four times higher than local sources.

When they met with potential buyers, they were determined to make the impression that although the price was high, the quality was excellent—and the service, world-class. When buyers balked, the firm was happy to recommend some competitive limestone suppliers with lower prices.

Meanwhile, during the course of the show, the representatives from the limestone firm met a young, affable Chinese salesman, whom they decided to hire *not* on a commission basis but on a full-time, salaried basis. His job was to show that the firm was committed to staying in the market. He was instructed not to push for a quick sale, but instead to conduct follow-up development on the leads from the show. To build relationships. To build trust.

The limestone makers were patient. They received requests for samples, which they produced perfectly. When one company wanted to give them a major order, the principal from the firm flew out for two consecutive meetings to cement the deal. When a container was said to have defective items, the principal flew out again to personally inspect and make good on whatever items had been destroyed.

That kind of personal service goes a long way in China, and customers began to buy this expensive limestone because of the service and support they knew they'd get from the firm. When you're buying limestone for a giant construction project, and you're importing tons of it, you want to know that your supplier is going to be reliable. Today, the limestone supplier's China business continues to grow briskly.

You may find, however, that an agent or distributor may be a good way to get a toehold in the market. You can always strike out on your own later. If that's the case, avoid signing exclusive deals with any agent. In order to distribute your product, you'll probably need several agents. And remember, an agent is not licensed to import. He's only allowed to sell. So he's one more step in the chain to consider.

SHOULD I SET UP AN OFFICE?

You should consider it. Especially if you're serious about doing business in China. Ninety-five percent of all inbound capital goes into three corporate forms: the representative office, the wholly owned foreign enterprise (WOFE), and the joint venture (JV), each with its own benefits and drawbacks, legal and economic requirements.

Representative Offices

Rep offices are the easiest to set up but have the most limited range of activity. They are not allowed to conduct any commerce. They can't sign contracts, invoice customers, or supply goods or services. But having such an office will put you in greater control of your sales and operational team.

Therefore, many U.S. firms have opted for this corporate form when starting out. The advantages? There's no capital investment required, there's a short setup period (one to two months), there's flexibility to exit, and you have full control of governance. The disadvantages? The scope of your business activities is restricted, and there are some rigid labor regulations (such as having to use government human resource agents). It's also not very tax-efficient.

Joint Ventures

The joint venture (JV) used to be the corporate form most foreign businesses chose—before WTO liberalized ownership rules. Today, the foreign partner must contribute a minimum of 25 percent of the registered capital in a JV. The Chinese JV partner usually contributes land and infrastructure to the enterprise.

The advantages? You've got immediate access to local knowledge, government relationships, and, hopefully, local management expertise. You also have the benefit of piggybacking on domestic brands or distribution channels that have already been built.

The disadvantages, however, are several. There are significant setup costs involved. The minimum foreign contribution to investment is $100,000. You also run into a big risk of clashing with your Chinese partner on management style and corporate culture, as well as on conflicts of interest that may emerge.

Make no mistake: your Chinese partner will determine the success or failure of your joint venture. A good partner will be able to help you navigate China's complex business environment. A bad partner will put you in the ground. Most investors complain about their partners stealing intellectual property, opening a rival company, or embezzling funds.

If you are considering a joint venture partner, make sure to spend a long time—more than you think is necessary—getting to know one another.

Wholly Owned Foreign Enterprises

Since WTO, 70 percent of all new foreign investments go into this corporate form. The advantages to establishing a wholly owned foreign enterprise (WOFE) are several: you've got full control over management, operations, and business strategy, it's easier to repatriate profits, and you benefit from better intellectual property rights protection.

The disadvantages? It's expensive (a minimum of about $120,500 registered capital). And it will probably take you longer to gain market access and local knowledge.

There are four types of licenses that a WOFE can do business under: wholesale (trading), which has its own import and export rights; manufacturing; retailing; and consulting/services.

WOFEs are subject to a few special incentives and goodies under the law:

- A Chinese national cannot own a WOFE.
- Profits are tax-free for the first two years of operation.
- There is only 7.5 percent tax on profits for the next three years (thereafter, a WOFE pays standard taxes on profits of 15 percent in Shenzhen and 30 percent outside of Shenzhen).
- A WOFE can get both import and export licenses, which other Chinese companies cannot.
- A WOFE can import one forty-foot container of personal articles duty-free, which can include vehicles, household articles, and so on.

- A WOFE engaged in manufacturing can import all its component parts and materials duty-free, so long as the production is exported later.
- Newer pieces of the law allow a WOFE to be a wholesale exporter, retailer, auctioneer, or commodities broker as well.
- A WOFE is allowed to export on its own licenses; there is no need to engage in the typical China practice of paying 1.5 to 4 percent of all invoiced costs in order to ship by "borrowing" export licenses from others (or shipping through a foreign trade company).
- And finally, a WOFE can keep multicurrency and foreign currency bank accounts in China. No other type of Chinese entity is permitted to do this. Also, the books, records, and accounting standards of a WOFE can be in any language and format you choose, so long as your government filings are in Chinese.

But you can't start up a WOFE in just any business. "Restricted" or "sensitive" industries still require a JV partner to enter the market. So you need to make sure you don't fall into one of these categories. Here is an abbreviated list of industries that are either restricted (companies must demonstrate their benefit to China) or prohibited (industries are deemed to be in the national security interests of the country and are off-limits). Some of the items may surprise you.

CATALOG OF RESTRICTED
FOREIGN INVESTMENT INDUSTRIES

Farming, Forestry, Animal Husbandry, and Fishery Industries

1. Development and production of grain (including potatoes), cotton, and oilseed (Chinese partner shall hold the majority of shares)
2. Processing of the logs of precious varieties of trees (equity joint ventures or contractual joint ventures only)

Mining and Quarrying Industries

1. Exploring and mining of minerals such as wolfram, tin, antimony, molybdenum, barite, and fluorite (equity joint ventures or contractual joint ventures only)
2. Exploring and mining of precious metals (gold, silver, platinum families)
3. Exploring and mining of precious nonmetals such as diamonds
4. Exploring and mining of special and rare kinds of coal (Chinese partner shall hold the majority of shares)
5. Mining of szaibelyite and szaibelyite iron ores
6. Mining of celestine

Manufacturing Industries

1. Food Processing Industry
   1.1 Production of millet wine and spirits of famous brands
   1.2 Production of soda beverages of foreign brand
   1.3 Production of synthetic sweet agents such as saccharin
   1.4 Processing of fat or oil
2. Tobacco Processing Industry
   2.1 Production of cigarettes and filter tips
3. Textile Industry
   3.1 Wool spinning, cotton spinning
   3.2 Silk reeling
4. Printing and Record Medium Reproduction Industry
   4.1 Printing of publications (Chinese partner shall hold the majority of shares except printing of package decoration)
5. Petroleum Processing and Coking Industries
   5.1 Construction and management of refineries
6. Chemical Raw Material and Products Manufacturing Industry
   6.1 Production of ionic membrane caustic soda
   6.2 Production of sensitive materials

6.3 Production of Benzedrine

6.4 Production of chemical products from which narcotics arc easily made (ephedrine, 3, 4-idene dihydro phenyl-2-acetone, phenylacetic acid, 1-phenyl-2-acetone, heliotropin, safrole, isosafrole, acetic oxide)

6.5 Production of sulphuric acid basic titanium white

6.6 Processing of baron, magnesium, iron ores

6.7 Barium salt production

7. Medical and Pharmaceutical Products Industry

7.1 Production of chloramphenicol, penicillin G, lincomycin, gentamicin, dihydrostreptomycin, amikacin, tetracycline hydrochloride, oxytetracycline, medemycin, kitasamycin, ilotyin, ciprofioxacin and offoxacin

7.2 Production of analgin, paracetamol, Vitamin B1, Vitamin B2, Vitamin C, Vitamin E

7.3 Production of immunity vaccines, bacterins, antitoxins and anatoxins (BCG vaccine, poliomyelitis, DPT vaccine, measles vaccine, Type-B encephalitis, and epidemic cerebrospinal meningitis vaccine) that are included in the State's Plan

7.4 Production of material medicines for addiction to narcotic and psychoactive drugs (Chinese partner shall hold the majority of shares)

7.5 Production of blood products

7.6 Production of non-self-destructible expendable injectors, transfusion systems, blood transfusion systems, blood bags

8. Chemical Fiber Production Industry

8.1 Production of chemical fiber drawnwork of conventional chipper

8.2 Production of viscose staple fiber with an annual single-thread output capacity of less than 20,000 tons

8.3 Production of polyester and spandex used for fiber and non-fiber with a daily production capacity of less than 400 tons

9. Rubber Products

   9.1 Cross-ply and old tire reconditioning (not including radial tires), and production of industrial rubber fittings of low performance

10. Nonferrous Metal Smelting and Rolling Processing Industry

   10.1 Smelting and separation of rare earth metals (equity joint ventures or contractual joint ventures only)

11. Ordinary Machinery Manufacturing Industry

   11.1 Manufacture of containers

   11.2 Manufacture of small and medium type ordinary bearings

   11.3 Manufacture of truck cranes of less than 50 tons (equity joint ventures or contractual joint ventures only)

12. Special Purpose Equipment Manufacturing Industry

   12.1 Production of low- or middle-class type-B ultrasonic displays

   12.2 Manufacture of equipment for producing long dacron thread

   12.3 Manufacture of crawler dozers of less than 320 horsepower, wheeled mechanical loaders of less than 3 cubic meter (equity joint ventures or contractual joint ventures only)

13. Electronic and Telecommunication Equipment Manufacturing Industry

   13.1 Production of satellite television receivers and key parts

Production and Supply of Power, Gas, and Water

1. Construction and operation of conventional coal-fired power plants whose unit installed capacity is less than 300,000kW (with the exception of small power grid)

Communication and Transportation, Storage, Post, and Telecommunication Services

1. Road passenger transportation companies
2. Cross-border automobile transportation companies

3. Water transportation companies

4. Railway freight transportation companies

5. Railway passenger transportation companies (Chinese partner shall hold the majority of shares)

6. General aviation companies engaging in photographing, prospecting, and industry (Chinese partner shall hold the majority of shares)

7. Telecommunication companies

Wholesale and Retail Trade Industries

1. Commercial companies of commodity trading, direct selling, mail order selling, Internet selling, franchising, commissioned operations, sales agents, commercial management companies, and wholesale and retail cotton, vegetable oil, sugar, medicines, tobaccos, automobiles, crude oil, capital goods for agricultural production

2. Wholesale or retail business of books, newspaper, and periodicals

3. Distributing and selling of audiovisual products (excluding movies)

4. Commodity auctions

5. Goods leasing companies

6. Agencies (ship, freight forwarding, tally for foreign vessels, advertising)

7. Wholesaling product oil, and construction and operation of gasoline stations

8. Foreign trade companies

Banking and Insurance Industries

1. Banks, finance companies, trust investment companies

2. Insurance companies

3. Security companies, security investment fund management companies

4. Financial leasing companies

5. Foreign exchange brokerage

6. Insurance brokerage companies

Real Estate Industry

1. Development of pieces of land (equity joint ventures or contractual joint ventures only)

2. Construction and operation of high-ranking hotels, villas, high-class office buildings, and international exhibition centers

Social Service Industry

1. Public Facility Service Industries

   1.1 Construction and operation of networks of gas, heat, water supply, and water drainage in large and medium-sized cities (Chinese partner shall hold the majority of shares)

2. Information, Consultation Service Industries

   2.1 Legal consulting

Public Health, Sports, and Social Welfare Industries

1. Medical treatment establishments (equity joint ventures or contractual joint ventures only)

2. Construction and operation of golf courses

Education, Culture, and Arts, Broadcasting, Film, and TV Industries

1. Education establishments for senior high school students (equity joint ventures or contractual joint ventures only)

2. Construction and operation of cinemas (Chinese partner shall hold the majority of shares)

Scientific Research and Polytechnical Services Industries

1. Mapping companies (Chinese partner shall hold the majority of shares)
2. Inspection, verification, and attestation companies for imported and exported goods

Other industries restricted by the State or international treaties that China has concluded or taken part in

CATALOGUE OF PROHIBITED FOREIGN INVESTMENT INDUSTRIES

Farming, Forestry, Animal Husbandry, and Fishery Industries

1. Cultivation of China's rare precious breeds (including fine genes in plants industry, husbandry, and aquatic products industry)
2. Production and development of genetically modified plants' seeds
3. Fishing in the sea area within government jurisdiction and in inland water

Mining and Quarrying Industries

1. Exploring, mining, and dressing of radioactive mineral products
2. Exploring, mining, and dressing of rare earth metal

Manufacturing Industry

1. Food Processing Industry
   1.1 Processing of green tea and special tea with China's traditional crafts (famous tea, dark tea, etc.)
2. Medical and Pharmaceutical Products Industry
   2.1 Processing of traditional Chinese medicines that have been listed as state-protected resources (musk, licorice, jute, etc.)

2.2 Application of preparing technique of traditional Chinese medicines in small pieces ready for decoction, and production of the products of secret recipes of traditional Chinese patent medicines

3. Nonferrous Metal Smelting and Rolling Processing Industry

   3.1 Smelting and processing of radioactive mineral products

4. Manufactures of Weapons and Ammunition

5. Other Manufacturing Industries

   5.1 Ivory carving

   5.2 Tiger-bone processing

   5.3 Production of bodiless lacquerware

   5.4 Production of enamel products

   5.5 Production of Xuan paper (rice paper) and ingot-shaped tablets of Chinese ink

   5.6 Production of carcinogenic, teratogenic, mutagenic, and persistent organic pollutant products

Production and Supply of Power, Gas, and Water

1. Construction and operation of power networks

Communication and Transportation, Storage, Post, and Telecommunication Services

1. Companies of air traffic control

2. Companies of postal services

Finance, Insurance Industries

1. Futures companies

Other Industries

1. Projects that endanger the safety and performance of military facilities

Did you notice how many industries are considered "sensitive"? Ad agencies. Banks. Insurance companies. All of these require a joint venture partner—and each category will have its own ownership rules. Over time, the restrictive regulations will most likely evolve, as China comes to understand the economic importance of the services sector. Then many of these industries may well be subject to tax incentives and other goodies to help you sell your wares.

WHAT ABOUT FRANCHISING?

When Dairy Queen entered the China market in 1992, they thought their biggest challenge would be to teach Chinese to enjoy their dessert treats. Little did they know that navigating China's franchising laws would prove even more difficult.

DQ, in the end, concluded that the laws were too complex to go it alone and decided to grant a Hong Kong company the master franchise to operate the subfranchises in China. DQ has found that their current setup has been much easier to manage. In general, franchising is a viable option to pursue, as restrictions on ownership, number of outlets, and geographical limitations on franchisers have all been eliminated. But be cognizant of the fact that you will be entering a very complex area of Chinese regs.

WHAT ABOUT LICENSING?

Licensing can be a good way to enter the market in some cases. It requires little capital and can provide you with good short-term benefits. However, be wary of the pitfalls of technology transfer. You may be creating your own competitor. Some companies counter this risk by licensing older technology to their Chinese partners, with an expectation of providing higher-level access at some future time or after a joint commercial milestone has been achieved.

If you are licensing technology, you also need to make sure that you're not trespassing on the U.S. export regime and should confirm whether the transfer of your technology is restricted. Your China licensing contract will also need to be approved by China's Ministry of Commerce. A tax of 10 to 20 percent (depending on the technology involved and the existing applicable bilateral tax treaty) will be withheld on royalty payments.

WHAT ABOUT ADVERTISING AND PROMOTION?

If the big Western shops subcontract work to local shops, is it a good idea to go direct yourself? Well, you'll pay a lot less. And a local shop might have good ideas on how to disseminate a message to a local audience. But they might not have the resources or the clout to execute. Local shops are small, and often have only one creative director and one account executive on the team.

In addition to more resources, you'll find the big agencies have much more leverage and reach on ad buys. Big shops will also tend to have better local research, as they place a premium on it, whereas local shops tend not to.

The predominant advertising channel is television. Eighty-four percent of China's 1.3 billion people are considered regular television viewers![14] Many companies are already trying to hawk their goods and services, including liquor, electronics, food, and toiletries, on TV.

Television stations in major markets require advertisers to make insertion orders two to ten months in advance. Newspapers and periodicals also deliver a broad audience, but their distribution is highly fragmented, making your media plan costly and complicated. For local (not national) campaigns, print media is a good alternative or complement to television.

Take note that certain copy techniques are not allowed, such as comparison advertising and using superlatives to describe your product. There are also regulations that require the verification of product safety and hygiene by the appropriate governing ministries. Censorship standards vary throughout China.

In addition to television, Internet adoption is rising in China. Online advertising is another viable option. You'll run into trouble with supporting online payments or delivering products, though, so it's better to think of your Internet ads and Web sites as online billboards for the time being, until the IT infrastructure and user sophistication catches up.

If you are trying to apply direct marketing techniques to your advertising and promotion, know that China is on the ground floor, lacking accurate lists and customer data. Although that's frustrating, the dearth of direct marketing infrastructure can serve as a big advantage to U.S. firms, which can build their own lists and mine those assets over the life of their customer relationships.

WHAT ABOUT DIRECT SELLING?

Avon is the primary direct seller in China. They entered the market in 1990. After large pyramid schemes in Beijing involving foot products bilked investors, sellers, and purchasers, and riots broke out, the government banned all direct selling for several years.[15]

When China joined the WTO, the government agreed to allow direct selling again. China had three years to implement regulations but was late to do so. The recently released regulations (which require U.S. businesses to have a minimum of three years' operating experience outside China) most likely are direct violations of WTO agreements.[16] Discussions are ongoing between the Office of the U.S. Trade Representative (USTR) and China on this issue. Avon was the first company to be officially granted a license to operate direct selling, on March 2, 2006. The jury is still out on how Avon will fare.

Avon's revenues today are growing again; they reported sales of 2.4 billion yuan in 2003, four times higher than before pyramid selling was banned. Amway's business volume, in turn, increased 120-fold from 1998 to 2003.

But these conditions were hard-won. Direct sales make the government nervous. They see them as building a "cultlike" atmosphere. So as a general rule, companies must have good relations with the government to be permitted a license for direct selling.

WHAT ABOUT SELLING
TO THE CHINESE GOVERNMENT?

Although the government states that they are trying to make procurement more transparent, that's not really happening. Projects that are funded by international organizations are almost always by open invitation, whereas most government projects are still by invitation only. Negotiation, not direct bidding, determines the outcome, behind closed doors.

Sales to the Chinese military and other government entities are regulated by both U.S. and Chinese law. U.S. manufacturers should contact the Department of Commerce's Bureau of Industry and Security and the U.S. State Department Office of Defense Trade Controls before attempting to sell goods or technology to the Chinese government or military.

HOW SHOULD I PRICE?

Given all the reasons they have to save their money (like health care), Chinese are slow to part with a yuan. Most Chinese consumers are sensitive to price and will tend to opt for the less expensive product, unless they perceive extra value either in quality or after-sales support. In the case of larger purchases, European and Japanese competitors sometimes offer layaway financing, which makes U.S. products less competitive.

Several factors should inform your pricing strategy:

Tariffs

Exports to China from the United States are assessed at a preferential rate—most-favored-nation status—because of membership in the WTO. In addition, special economic zones, foreign trade zones, and open cities provide further reductions and exemptions. There are a great many of these special zones.

Here is a list of the Economic and Technology Development Zones.*

Beijing	Huangshi	Suzhou Industrial Park
Changan Technology Park	Jiangning	Suzhou New District
Chengdu	Kunming	Tainjin
Chongqing	Kunshan	Urumqi
Dalian	Minhang	Weihai
Daya Bay	Nansha	Wenzhou
Dongshan	Nantong	Wuhan
Fuzhou	Ningbo	Wuhu
Guangzhou	Pudong New District	Xhenyang
Hainan Yangpu	Qingdao	Xiamen Haicang
Hangzhou	Qinghuangdao	Xi'an
Harbin	Shanghai Caohejing	Xiaoshan
Hefei	Shanghai Jinqiao	Yingkou
Hohhot	Shanghai Lujiazui	Zhengzhou

Before deciding to go into business in a particular area, check first if there is a special economic zone there. Chances are there will be. If you set up shop there, you'll be eligible for preferential rates on tariffs and other tax benefits.

Also, China sometimes applies tariff rates that are significantly lower than the published most-favored-nation rate, when it is trying to

*For more economic and technology zones, visit AllTheT.com/SEZ.

stimulate the development of an industry that it deems important. For example, China has slashed tariffs on steel, chemicals, and automotive parts. Food, wine, and cosmetics are other categories whose tariffs are being reduced. Keeping an eye on tariff rates is a good way to determine what industries China is supporting with incentives.

China's harmonized tariff system is also still evolving. Before 2004, China was using eight-digit codes to classify its harmonized tariff system instead of the more detailed ten-digit codes that the United States uses. Without this level of specificity, Chinese customs officials had a lot more discretion in classifying what general category your product fell into, and therefore how much it was assessed. Today, ten-digit codes are used to classify some items, including chemicals, internal combustion engines, rare earth, pumps, and automobiles, and that's tightened things up quite a bit.

Customs Valuation

China customs officials are tasked with evaluating all imports in terms of a fair valuation. They use a valuation database that lists pricing for products based on international and domestic markets. The prices that you assert on your forms are the prices that the customs officials compare with the database. Usually, customs will go with the importer's price, unless the price is so far out of line with the database that the official then estimates the goods' value based on a predetermined formula. If you don't nail down your customs valuation in advance, you could get hit with an unexpected duty that could impact your margin, so price accordingly.

Taxes

The two taxes you're going to need to pay are value-added taxes (VAT) and corporate taxes. VAT is assessed after the tariff and reflects the value of the tariff. Although WTO rules mandate that goods produced by domestic Chinese firms and imported goods must be treated the same according to taxation, importers complain that their local competitors are often exempt from paying VAT at the border.

The general VAT rate is 17 percent, but necessities, such as agricultural products, fuel, and utility items, are taxed at 13 percent. Small businesses get more favorable treatment, and their tax burden is less.

VAT rebates up to a full 17 percent are available for processed exports. But exporters report that realizing the rebates takes months, and the amounts are usually wrong. Funds are limited by local budgets, and in the coastal cities, money often runs out before the end of the year.

The primary corporate tax for companies operating in China is an income tax, which varies depending on the type of corporate ownership.

WHAT ABOUT CUSTOMER SERVICE AND AFTER-SALES SUPPORT?

Ironically, even though Chinese firms are deficient in this area, foreign firms are not permitted to provide after-sales and customer service support for products they sell into China. They can, however, provide these services for products that they make themselves in China.

Sometimes foreign firms partner with locals to provide service and spare parts. But many U.S. companies state that this leaves them with little control over the quality of the service, which is often a problem. They feel this erodes their brand equity. These companies, instead, choose to try to provide customer service and after-sales support from Hong Kong.

PITCHING NEW BUSINESS

If you're selling into China, you're going to be pitching your wares to an unfamiliar audience. The more pitches you do, the more you'll learn about your customers. But here are some tips that I've picked up along the way.

Be humble. Most Western firms overlook a very important part of winning business in China. They prepare for a month on the Power-Point deck until it's perfect. But the buyer is looking at the deck and also who's presenting it. Humility matters. Western firms make the mistake of walking into a room and thinking they can command respect. It doesn't work that way anymore. Arrogance will lose you the business.

Invest your time in preselling, not PowerPoint. Your Chinese competitors go out of their way to do homework on everybody. They find out the organizational chart. Who needs to look like a genius in front of the boss? Who are the decision makers? Who are the ones to be wary of?

A good first step toward learning this kind of information is to invest time in making the receptionist your friend. Bring her gifts. Talk to her. Find out about her family. Tell her about yours. The receptionists are the gatekeepers. They will give you access or shut you out. And they'll also help you with inside information, if you are kind and humble.

Be on time. Even if it's a rainy day, if you show up five minutes late, you're finished. It reflects badly on you. In addition to the receptionist, always bring gifts for the prospective clients.

Try to avoid asking direct questions. They will ask them of you. But your questions may put people on the spot and make your clients look bad in front of their boss. Ask indirect and modest questions. You can stomp around with big feet when you're a buyer—not when you're a seller.

Demonstrate how hard you work. Chinese respect that. Make it a point to get back to their requests very quickly, and keep fulfilling their expectations.

■

When an ostrich sticks his head in the sand, his tufty rump flips up high in the air. Not only does he suffer from the misguided perception

that by hiding from danger, he can avoid it—but he also looks positively ridiculous doing so.

I'm thinking of avian tuchises as I read this week's trade magazine
from one of the big industry associations. Article after article smears
China for a number of wrongs. The editorial slant is supported by
quotes from business owners, unions, and management—all united in
a hallelujah chorus of invective against China.

Yet I see nothing written anywhere about the bonanza of opportunities that present themselves to this industry—how exporters are already making a killing selling to China, building demand and opening
new markets. By doing so, they're helping to maintain America's primacy in the world and are contributing to China's stable evolution into
a modern economy.

But, aside from that, they're exacting the best revenge of all on a
lousy customer—selling them more goods and services! Better than
getting mad is getting even.

6

COMPETING WITH CHINA

Close the doors, they're coming through the windows!

"He did *what?!*" I can hear my partner's wrath through the wall. His door must be open again. We share office space with a law firm, and these frequent explosions elicit squirming and eye-rolling by the legal secretaries who sit in the cubbies along the corridor.

I'll go shut the door. The opera singer who moonlights as a temp is heaving dramatic sighs. Okay, okay. This isn't the final scene of *Aïda*.

My partner waves me in. I take a chair. He's on the phone to China. We pay a penny a minute for service, but it sounds like you're calling from a phone booth under the Tappan Zee Bridge. He is shouting. His face is round and red. I hunch in the chair and fan out my legs. And stiffen, suddenly remembering the lecture I once got on sloppy chair posture. The spine obediently straightens.

Waves of tritonal Mandarin crash over me. "*Bu, bu, bu, bu bu!*" (Translation: NO, NO, NO, NO, NO!) He's cursing loudly now. At his elbow is the picture of him and the Dalai Lama, two rapt faces captured in a moment of laughter. When visiting clients notice the picture, I explain that my partner is posing with our new marketing director. From where I'm sitting, I can see the lama's scarlet robes but can't make out the polo insignia on my partner's button-down, which I remember from closer inspections of the photo. The two garments were probably made in the same factory.

Third Avenue glints at me dully through long gray windows. We've moved our staff into offices at the Chrysler Building. Actually, the Chrysler *Center,* to be more precise—the boxy glass eyesore that abuts the back of the elegant landmark. Both Chrysler edifices share a lobby and a management company, but not an address. Regrettably, we're at 666 Third Avenue. Our clients never fail to razz us. We're clearly tainted by Satan. (Asserting that 666 in Chinese means good luck doesn't persuade them otherwise.)

I stretch. I see the dark walnut bookcases. They're lined not with yellowing law books but with bric-a-brac, a museum to our folly. There's the bronze eagle flag ornament. The black bite-block for oral surgery. The red, oblong taillight spilling wires. The music box that plays "Moon River"—my partner's favorite song. The grimy crank-shaft. Each product tells its tale of woe.

There's the wedding-cake figurine. An Asian bride grips the hand of a wheelchair-bound African-American groom. We'd made several sets of interchangeable couples with different ethnicities and states of physical health. Sadly, the buyer refused to pay for production molds, and the program was scrapped after we made samples. We were left with a box of little plastic wheelchairs and body parts. Bride's head re-visited. Here stands the last, lonely assembled pair.

I see the finials, stolid little caps made to crown a fence post. They're stacked atop one another and list dangerously sideways. The finials are made of compression-molded wood fiber. They have the look of wood but the durability of plastic. Getting the right propor-tion of plastic to pulp was critical. Once we discovered the right bal-ance, we failed to sell this product to the big-box retailers like Wal-Mart.

The goods are everywhere, strewn on bookshelves, tabletops, and windowsills. And inside the file cabinets are still more: granite slabs and surgical masks, medical tube fittings and sink faucets, shutoff valves and air conditioner grills. "Our black gold," my partner always calls them. A thick, mangled carpet of bills, research reports, and inky Chinese newspapers covers his desk.

He slams down the phone. We have problems. Apparently, one of our factories is trying to go around us—and is probably in league with an employee in our Ningbo office. Our client spotted their products at a Chinese trading company, stamped with a different brand. The evidence of foul play seemed unimpeachable. Our factory is selling goods out the back door.

Funny, I'd always thought that we'd get whacked from the other direction first—that U.S. clients would seek to go around us and do business directly with our Chinese factories. When investors asked us about this risk, we'd always say, "Let them go ahead with our blessings. Here are the phone numbers to the plant managers." In reality, none of our customers were thrilled at the idea of running multisupplier programs—which is why they hired us in the first place. But contracts with our clients sought to prevent this sort of circumvention anyway. For low-value, commodity products, the temptation to go around us would be real. As for our factories, that was a different matter. I didn't expect them to go around us; after all, we were delivering business to them and helping them modernize. Or at least, I didn't expect them to go around us so quickly.

China business veterans will cluck at me and say this happens all the time. They're right. Competition is so fierce in China that it goads companies to go head-to-head even with their Western customers. There's a cruel process of natural selection playing out among China's overcrowded industries. All the subscale companies left over from the days of Mao are clamoring for dominance over the burgeoning privately owned firms.

Competition is cutthroat among the labor force, as well. There are many more skilled workers in the marketplace than there are jobs to employ them. And to make matters worse, thousands of skilled work-ers are getting fired every month from the dying state-owned sector. If that weren't bad enough, it's become common practice to poach labor. (Although employment contracts exist, they're not readily enforced.)

Itinerant skilled employees and acquisitive companies make for a lethal combination. There's always a threat that one of your work-ers may walk out the door with a trade secret and take it to your competition.

Clearly, Chinese are accustomed to different rules of engagement. Business is business. If the difference between life or death means go-ing around your customer or hiring your competitor's staff, so be it. If it means copying your customer's technology, get out your pencils and start drafting. It's survival of the shiftiest.

PROTECTING YOUR TRADE SECRETS

How can you do business in such a place? If you talk to policy makers and academics about China's wanton disregard for intellectual prop-erty rights, they'll often throw up their hands and say it will take noth-ing short of a revolution to change China's system—or several generations of incremental reform.

That's not an answer you can take to the bank. So businesses are de-veloping their own techniques to protect their intellectual property in-country.

Reintermediation: The Multisupplier Option

U.S. cosmetics companies, when they first started sourcing goods in China, were shocked to find their brands emblazoned on inferior mer-chandise lining the shelves of Chinese retail. Their suppliers were copying their products and selling them out the back door. A supplier to Revlon, Estée Lauder, and Maybelline from Oxnard, California, shrewdly employs a method of protecting its intellectual property that has become standard operating procedure in the cosmetics industry. In order to manufacture a new line of makeup applicators in China, the company insisted on farming out the job to more suppliers than necessary—subcontracting the component parts to several factories on a need-to-know basis, so no single factory had the specifications for the entire, assembled product. By adding layers in the chain, they keep the secret of their design guarded.

Many China business veterans insist on taking these kinds of special precautions, especially in industries where design is fashion-driven, such as cosmetics and apparel, or where your technology is proprietary. (It's less of a concern, obviously, to producers of sink drains or pump gaskets.)

Turn Your Suppliers into Your Sales Force

Henry Schein, Inc.—the world's largest wholesaler of medical and dental supplies to doctors' offices—employs another very innovative approach. Schein doesn't manufacture anything. The vast book of products that they sell is procured and warehoused. Schein has hundreds of factories under management around the world, but especially in China.

The Long Island company takes a pragmatic view on their Chinese suppliers. They know that the temptation to copy their products and sell them in local markets will be great, especially as the health care industry is booming in China.

So rather than attempting to stick their fingers in the bursting dike, they instead harness that desire to sell. They turn their suppliers into their in-country sales partners. If the factories are going to try to sell anyway, why not formalize the process and provide sales support to help the factories penetrate Chinese markets? This arrangement has proven very successful so far. They align their suppliers' profit motives with their own.

Keep Your China Staff on a Need-to-Know Basis

Since turnover is so great in China, your staff is a sieve of sensitive information. Clued into your secrets, they're even more coveted by the competition. Take pains not to allow access by your employees to anything you consider sensitive.

Financials should be kept secret. In the West, financial statements are often shared with management, so as to align the team's operational goals with your business goals. In China, this is not always a good idea. If too many members of your China team know the inner financial workings of your business—your balance sheet, your margins— that information could be leaked to a competitor.

Client data should also be kept secret. If you are sourcing goods from China and reselling them to Western customers, for example, make sure that the names and addresses of these clients remain a secret. Once your China team knows the contact info of your customers, the temptation will be great to go around you and service those customers themselves, or bring the customers with them to another firm.

One precaution you can take is by coding your client list. You keep the master list, and the China team is provided the encoded list. So they never know who your end buyer is or their contact info.

These kinds of defensive maneuvers will help safeguard your secrets. Once you start doing business in-country, you'll discover some more of your own. In the meantime, bear in mind that while China still has a quite a long way to go, it is beginning to make progress in its protection of intellectual property.

Remember, some of the most significant inventions of the last few millennia were made in China. China invented money and gunpowder. Paper before the Egyptians. A printing press before the Gutenberg Bible.

But China hasn't produced a big hit in a long time. Seven hundred years of repressive government haven't helped. Wars, brutal subjugation by autocracies and invaders, and great famines have stifled innovation for centuries.

So China has had to bootstrap its modern economy not by innovating, but by *imitating*—by making cheaper what the world already consumes. China has not become the world's manufacturing and assembly hub because it has superior technologies. China, by and large, has inferior technologies. But if America's economic pioneers were great entrepreneurs, China's are great improvisers. They have learned very quickly to fulfill the needs of the world's most demanding customers with subpar equipment, personnel, and infrastructure.

A story from World War II is a good illustration. When General Curtis LeMay wanted to stage air sorties on Japan from Chinese bases, local laborers were employed to build runways for the U.S. planes. Lacking modern equipment, the Chinese improvised and set about crushing rocks into macadam with rollers that looked like giant ink blotters, requiring several people to push. Once in a while, a worker would slip under the roller and get crushed. The rest of the workers would giggle and keep going.

It's also important to note that the very notion of intellectual property is foreign to this (until recently) Marxist country. Things you make with your hands have owners. But, ideas? Most Chinese still struggle to comprehend this concept. Intellectual property rights in the West have evolved over the course of four hundred years of corporation law. Our cultures appreciate what these rights mean and why they're important. The Chinese don't, as yet.

But money talks in China, and the Chinese authorities know that if they can't protect intellectual property rights, money will walk. China, then, would lose its coveted status as the world's top destination of foreign direct investment, a position that until recently belonged to the United States.

You can see the government is making some strides, both through legislation and through enforcement in the courts. When Danish toy maker Lego discovered its China joint venture partner was making Lego knockoffs and selling them out the back door, Lego sued its partner and won an injunction in a local Chinese court. The Chinese factory was forced to destroy its molds and pay Lego restitution.

However, not all Western firms are finding China's courts hospitable. When American footwear maker New Balance discovered its shoes were being slovenly imitated and sold in China by its joint venture partner, the court ruled in favor of the Chinese party anyway.

China's measures still have much room for improvement. In a typical example, a system of special courts to hear intellectual property cases was established, but not special prosecutors. So the attorneys that handle intellectual property claims are usually unfamiliar with the complexities of Chinese intellectual property law.

Yet despite the relatively inhospitable climate, many U.S. and Japanese companies, such as Sony, are moving design labs to China. In fact, over seven hundred research and development centers were opened in China over the past couple years alone. Part of this trend reflects China's small gains in protecting intellectual property rights.

But while China strives for better courts, better enforcement, and better *understanding* among its citizens, Western companies doing business on the mainland should not rely on the system to protect intellectual property rights. You've got to aggressively defend your secrets through tactics like supplier reintermediation and restricting information flow.

HEAD-TO-HEAD ENTERPRISE COMPETITION

Trade secrets are one thing. But how can you defend yourself against Chinese competition? China's economy is a hothouse for world-class competitors. A company must capture only a fraction of the local market to achieve the scale needed to compete overseas. In some cases,

Chinese competitors entering the U.S. market will be beneficial. They will create jobs and build value. In other cases, U.S. businesses and labor should take to the ramparts.

The first important step in defending ourselves, though, is not to be afraid. Fear obfuscates the facts. Take the case in 2005 when Dubai Ports World sought to acquire the British-owned Peninsular & Oriental Steam Navigation Company, which would have put control of the terminal operations of six U.S. ports in the hands of a Dubai firm. The outcry in America from all quarters was venomous and largely fictional.

Politicians from both parties did not simply demand a stop to the deal. They advocated the immediate return of all American port operations to American hands—disregarding the small detail that 80 percent of the firms that run port terminal operations are already owned by foreigners.

Did they propose to seize these assets with the National Guard or by a militia of armed longshoremen? By eminent domain? By presidential fiat? Of course in reality, the idea is untenable. Yet serious, thoughtful people asserted these claims on the national airwaves.

Most of the pundits and politicians who made these remarks knew better. And they knew why American companies left this low-margin business to begin with. Running port terminals in the United States has become a mostly automated affair, and there's not much margin in it. The terminal operators do not *own* the ports; they own the rights only to operate the terminals, rights they must reapply for after their lease runs out.

But politicians realized they had discovered a deep vein of rage and fear among Americans, and by tapping it, they could extract a mother lode of political gold. They played to American xenophobia shamelessly. In reality, port security—the screening of containers, the inspection of cargo manifests, the clearance of goods—is handled exclusively by the U.S. government. While you might feel that the government could do more to protect our ports, the threat a terminal operator poses to American national security is minimal. Certainly, we were not outsourcing our port security to Dubai.

As if raising the specter of terrorism were not enough, they went on to evoke the "dreaded Chinese." (They really pulled out all the stops.) Chinese control of terminal operations in Long Beach, California, and the Panama Canal was drummed up frequently by media and politicians as a self-evident threat to our national security.

Let's take a step back for a moment. America still owns America. The market value of foreign assets in the United States totals about $3 trillion. Our gross domestic product for 2006 was about $12.5 trillion. That means the market value of foreign-owned assets in the United States is about 20 percent of the value of goods and services we produce *in a single year.* This is not the picture of a country whose assets are owned lock, stock, and barrel by foreigners.

Who are the invading Visigoths? The United Kingdom is the largest foreign owner of American enterprises, followed by Japan, Germany, the Netherlands, and France. China's holdings in U.S. companies is less than $5 billion.

In fact, corporate merger and acquisition activity in the United States is still dominated by American firms buying other American firms. In 2005, there were 7,298 M&As. Just 936 American companies were acquired by foreigners. (Five thousand, two hundred and seventy-four M&As were U.S. firms acquiring other U.S. firms, and 1,088 were American firms buying foreign firms.)[1]

In some undeniable ways, foreign investment is good for our economy—for both labor and business. For instance, foreign-owned companies on American soil employ about 5.3 million Americans. These workers, on average, earn 34 percent more than their counterparts in U.S.-owned firms. From a macroeconomic perspective, though, many economists believe that these inflows of foreign investment are not just beneficial, but critical to the security of our economy. Our global trade deficit was $725 billion in 2005. We need capital inflows, like foreign direct investment, to help bring our accounts into balance and keep the economy solvent.

Of course, this doesn't mean we should sell off our key assets—especially those linked to national security—just to stay economically healthy. Appropriately, there's a government body whose job is to police potential foreign investments in the United States and their impact on national security. It's called CFIUS (pronounced *SIH-fius*), the Committee on Foreign Investment in the United States, and it advises the president on which deals should go through and which should be blocked on the grounds of national security.

CFIUS was established in 1975. But the notion of linking foreign direct investment and national security was not new. When a German diplomat forgot his briefcase on a train platform in 1915, U.S. officials learned that German investments in America were helping build its war machine back home. President Wilson later seized these assets when the United States entered World War I. Later, in 1927, fearing Communist infiltration into the nation's communications infrastructure, Congress blocked foreign ownership of radio broadcasting assets.

These days, we worry about acquirers that are controlled by foreign governments—the inference being that a foreign government might wish to act against U.S. interests through its corporate surrogates operating on our shores. Law requires CFIUS to conduct a thorough review of any deal involving such a company.

Not that this kind of situation happens frequently, mind you. Only about 2 percent of foreign holdings in the United States are owned by state-run companies. Dubai Ports World, which is government controlled, should have triggered such an investigation, but it did not.

Many, therefore, accuse CFIUS of sleeping at the switch. CFIUS has received more than 1,500 notifications since 1988; it conducted a full investigation of just twenty-five cases. Of these cases, thirteen were withdrawn when told they'd be subject to a full review (the business equivalent to a body cavity search), and the other twelve were sent on to the president. Of these twelve, just one potential acquisition was blocked. In 1990, after Tiananmen Square, President George H. W. Bush stopped a Chinese company's attempted purchase of an aircraft parts manufacturer—the only rejection in CFIUS history.[2]

Americans will probably be relieved to hear that most foreign ownership today is concentrated in nonsensitive areas of the U.S. manufacturing sector. For example: Lenovo of China purchased IBM's PC division for $1.75 billion in 2005; Shanghai Haixin Group bought Glenoit Corp Specialty Fabrics in 2002 for $14 million; and Huayi Group of Shanghai bought Moltech Power Systems for an estimated $20 million in 2002. These are the typical sorts of foreign direct investment transactions that occur.

However, some foreign ownership does extend into sensitive sectors. Venezuela's state-owned Citgo, as well as British Petroleum of the United Kingdom and Royal Dutch Shell of the Netherlands, own assets in the U.S. energy sector. In telecommunications, Sweden's Ericsson and Finland's Nokia have holdings here. In food, France's Sodexho USA is the largest food service company in the United States, even serving meals on Marine Corps bases. The largest private security firm operating in the United States is Sweden's Securitas.

So while foreign companies do control assets in the United States, and some of these holdings lie in sensitive industries, we are a long way from a national crisis, as some fear. The country hasn't been sold out to foreigners, and the infrastructure that protects our security remains intact.

WHAT KIND OF COMPETITION CAN WE EXPECT?

American industry faces two forms of Chinese competition: direct investment, when Chinese companies buy their way into our markets; and shifting comparative advantage, as jobs and capital flow to China when it's easier and cheaper to buy from them than produce ourselves. Both onslaughts can be countered with a little foresight, turning challenges into opportunities.

I look back at my partner. I'm dumbfounded. Wait a second, I stammer, our client found their products—*stamped with another brand*—being sold by a Chinese trading company? This would put the entire account at risk. He starts reciting the punishments he will mete out to our employee, whom he suspects is colluding with the factory.

I am more concerned with the factory itself; we're running a number of other orders at this plant. If the owner screwed us on this deal, what's to prevent him from screwing us on others? I suggest that we cease doing business with him and move all the molds from the factory floor immediately. "Silly boy," my partner says with his flat stare. He reminds me that the factory has leverage over us. Though we technically own the molds, the factory will certainly resist moving them and disrupt all of our runs in progress, should we threaten to remove them ourselves.

How can we keep our factories from trying to go around us? Contracts certainly don't help. Our best defense is to keep as close to our customer as possible, making sure that we are adding much more value than the mere purveying of cheap goods.

Direct Investment

I learned that day how Chinese competitors may try to go around you and sell to *your* customer. Or they may pursue the direct investment route, in which they will seek to purchase a controlling interest in a U.S. firm. (In this case, the United Nations defines a controlling interest as owning 10 percent or more of a company's stock or voting rights.)

Forward-leaning companies in China have a number of reasons to invest in the United States: most notably, America's large, affluent markets and favorable business regulations. These, in fact, are the top reasons Chinese firms give for investing in the United States. Not surprisingly, then, America has been the second-largest recipient of Chinese direct investment since 1979.

But the barriers to market entry are high. In order to succeed in the United States, businesses must have a command of the softer skills of commerce: branding, sales, marketing, and customer services—areas in which Chinese firms generally lag far, far behind.

Americans worried about Chinese competitors will also be relieved to hear that any competitive advantage these firms may have had on their own turf vanishes once they enter our markets. Their edge in pricing, brand awareness, human resources, technology, distribution, financing, and market research—all these disappear in the United States.[3]

In an exhaustive survey the World Bank conducted of Chinese companies that invest overseas, over half of these firms reported the dire need for consulting services to help them survive in the West. These firms are hiring consultants in risk analysis and management, strategic planning and brand development, taxation, auditing, accounting, industry analysis, and market research. If you're working in any of those services, Chinese companies operating on American shores can be a good source of new business for you.

Foreign competition cuts two ways. The most lethal competitors sometimes do the most good for the economy and for the job market. The phenomenon is called "insourcing"—when foreign companies invest in America and add jobs to our economy.

The Haier Group (pronounced "Hire"), China's leading white

goods manufacturer, is serving such a purpose. Haier's expansion in the States has been good news for labor and management.

To give you an idea of Haier's size, picture this: in 2003, they sold more than 5 million refrigerators—that's 7 percent of the world's demand and 26 percent of China's demand. The total U.S. market is about 10 million refrigerators per year, and GE sold approximately 3.5 million units in 2003. So by servicing just 26 percent of China's domestic demand, Haier is already ranked the fifth-largest white goods company in the world.

Haier bought a New York landmark to serve as U.S. HQ (a former bank, the building expresses the attribute of permanence). It's a move that shows they understand some of the nuances of branding. They're also investing heavily in U.S. plants, equipment, personnel, and design labs (such as their design lab in Boston). Haier's hiring. U.S. staffing comprises both labor and management, providing jobs in the white goods industry, which has been hard hit in recent years.

The Haier Group's entry strategy rests on its belief that contract manufacturing, in and of itself, is a low-value function that lacks true competitive difference in the marketplace and therefore cannot support expansion into Western markets. Instead, Haier seeks to control its own distribution network and is investing heavily in research and development.

This is a gutsy and expensive strategy, and many Chinese eyes are watching. If Haier succeeds, it will serve as a model for others. Some TV manufacturers are trying the same ploy: Konka Electronics, Skyworth, and Changhong Electronics Group are buying their way into the U.S. market. They are also creating American jobs in a sector that has seen intense competition from Chinese imports.

But buying their way into the U.S. market is expensive and risky. Partnering is arguably a safer way for Chinese companies to enter, and many firms are choosing this strategy instead. For example, the merger of the television and DVD operations of China's TCL with France's Thompson allows TCL to gain instant brand equity and distribution in the West, selling under the Thompson brand in Europe and the RCA brand in the United States.

Similarly, Huawei Electronics, China's largest manufacturer of telecom equipment, has partnered with U.S.-based 3Com to expand into the data networking services market. The alliance lets Huawei piggyback on 3Com's U.S. and European distribution network (and lets 3Com have access to the Chinese market). Given the fact that big Chinese companies often sell multiple product lines, this hybrid approach is probably one we'll see a lot more of over time.

How Do You Know If a Chinese Entrant Is on the Horizon?

The best way to tell if a Chinese competitor is gunning for you is to keep vigil not just on what they're doing—but also on what we're doing. Watch China's markets, but also watch for breaches where Chinese competition can penetrate.

Watching China's Markets

People who live in hurricane zones often track storms over Africa before they gather strength in the Atlantic and whack the eastern seaboard. You can do the same with Chinese markets. The industries are starting to shake out: smaller players are being crushed, and dominant firms are growing and consolidating.

Stay on top of the trends by consulting the many Chinese business publications online that are translated into English. You don't need to follow the minutiae. What you're really keeping an eye on is the clash of the titans—the competitive shake-out among China's largest companies. Overcrowding afflicts China's large market firms, just as it does the small and middle markets. So the same brutal natural selection process is going on among the giants.

As the shakeout continues, we can expect to see large Chinese firms

Number of Large Chinese Manufacturers by Industry

Air conditioners	300
Apparel	9,000
Commercial trucks	25
Construction equipment	85
Mobile phones	37
Passenger cars	30
Pharmaceuticals	3,000
Steel	1,000

Source: China Statistical Yearbook, SAIC, Off-Highway Research, December 31, 2003

in many industries attempt to set up operations in the United States.*
Characteristics of U.S. industries provide clues to whether they are vulnerable to Chinese competition.

Watching Our Markets

Keep an eye on the following market traits within your own industry
to assess the threat level:

BRAND LOYALTY: Chinese companies lack brand awareness in the
United States. No one has heard of them here, and the Mandarin
names often sound strange. Plus, they're much less adept at building
their brands than American firms are. Therefore, markets in which
brand loyalty plays less of a role in guiding purchase decisions are exposed to potential Chinese competition. Industrial and corporate buyers, for example, place less faith in brands as an indicator of quality
than retail consumers do, preferring instead to conduct in-depth due
diligence. So if you sell products and services to businesses, watch
your back.

*For more China industry breakdowns, visit AllTheT.com/industries.

AFTER-SALES SUPPORT: Chinese firms usually lack comprehensive after-sales support, as it demands both soft skills and sophisticated logistics. So industries that require little after-sales support are exposed to Chinese competition. Consumer electronics, for example, is an industry that will surely face Chinese heat.

SEGMENTED MARKETS: If your markets are segmented by price, Chinese competitors may try to compete on the bottom of the product mix, where lower prices may motivate customers to switch. Both Japan and South Korea employed this strategy to enter U.S. markets; they then worked their way up the value chain from the low to the high end in consumer electronics and automobiles. We can expect to see China try to take the same path.

PRODUCT LIFE: Products that are replaced frequently, like mobile phones, give competitors more opportunities to capture market share. If a cell phone is replaced about every two years, your competition gets five looks over the course of a decade. Compare that to construction equipment, which usually is replaced every five to ten years. In that industry, competitors only have at most two shots a decade to penetrate.

PROFIT MARGINS: If margins are healthy at home, Chinese firms will have less incentive to compete overseas. Construction equipment in China has been booming, for example, and the margins have been lush. So even though segments of the market are fragmented (there are eighty-five makers of wheeled loaders in China, for example), everybody is still making good money. But in the next cyclical downturn, some of these companies may be forced to look overseas for more business—and China's construction equipment industry has weaned some large players.

■

I emerge from my partner's office and close the door behind me, lest another volcanic phone call erupt. The opera singer is at lunch anyway. My head is swimming. What will I tell our customer? An apology would be a good place to start. I've started concocting one in my head when my partner calls a staff meeting.

We all file into a conference room. He's got a sheaf of papers in his hand. I can see the title on the top page. It's a contract I recently prepared, a confidentiality agreement that prohibits both disclosing trade secrets and soliciting our factories, clients, or employees. My partner distributes them like a math test. Take one, and pass it down. Six of us obey.

I see what he's doing. Signed confidentiality agreements in the Ningbo office may be unenforceable, but in New York, it's a different story. He is trying to fortify our ramparts. He's quite right. These contracts should have been signed a long time ago. I'm delighted he's taken a sudden shine to legal affairs.

At the inception of the company, his disdain for legal services was immediately apparent—and something I should have anticipated from one who grew up in a country where business is carried out mostly on an informal basis. As the son of a lawyer, I tend to take a different view, especially as I'm not an attorney myself. I advocated that we hire a lawyer to help us get our corporate house in order: filings, by-laws, private placement documents.

Nonsense, I was told. Just fill this in—and he handed me a fat black binder. It was our corporate book—with all of the documents associated with establishing and governing the company left blank. "You've got to be kidding," I remember saying. If we messed this up, the foundation of the company would be unstable. We dug into a bruising discussion over the relevance of lawyers (the first of many), but he wouldn't budge an inch. I brought in a lawyer anyway as outside counsel—a friend at a large firm, who pitied me.

Everyone's head is bowed in reading. I allow a couple quiet minutes to pass and then try to offer some explanation of what they're looking at. The language is fairly standard. It defines what's deemed confidential and what's not. Should confidentiality be breached or our suppliers, customers, or employees solicited, the contract provides for our right to seek remedies.

There are nods. The pen is passed around. Everyone signs. I countersign. On my contract, my partner countersigns, and I do the same on his. As I look at the group, I wonder who will be the first to breach the contract.

SHIFTING COMPARATIVE ADVANTAGE

Chinese competitors will vie to go around you to get to your end customer, or they may try to buy their way into your market through direct investment. Or they'll just suck jobs and capital into their economy through asserting comparative advantage—an economic theory that describes why Country A trades with Country B, even if Country A has the ability to manufacture everything itself. Answer: Country A does so because it's cheaper and easier to trade with Country B than produce the goods domestically.

In some cases, comparative advantage derives from nature. Saudi Arabia sits on tremendous deposits of oil, for example; New York does not. But in many cases, comparative advantage is based on human effort, and in evolving economies, comparative advantage moves. England used to have a comparative advantage in textile manufacturing. That advantage shifted to New England, then to the Carolinas, then to Latin America, then to China and other low-wage manufacturing environments.

To predict a shift in comparative advantage, economists often lump industries into two broad categories: tradable, something that can be put in a box and shipped, and nontradable, something that is either too heavy to be shipped or is an intangible, like services. If something is tradable, so the logic goes, it's vulnerable to the dynamics of comparative advantage, and jobs and capital could move.

Of course, today those classifications are breaking down. Advances in logistics allow us to transport many more kinds of items over longer distances, and advances in technology allow us to trade many intangibles, like services, over information networks. So the industries that are vulnerable to a shift in comparative advantage (and therefore the outflow of jobs) number many more than might first have been imagined—in both the manufacturing and the services sectors.

Let's consider the manufacturing sector, for a moment, which employed 14.3 million Americans at the end of 2004. From an economist's perspective, since most of the goods produced by this sector are "tradable," they're vulnerable to a shift in comparative advantage.

While this may be true in the abstract, the reality is more nuanced; certain jobs must stay close to home. Some products just don't lend themselves well to shipping. Take appliances, for example. While component parts can easily be shipped, the large, open cavities found in refrigerators and other white goods are a highly wasteful and expensive use of a sea container. Other products must be built close to the site because they are either too large (homes) or cannot tolerate long-distance transport (perishables).

Often, comparative advantage may vary within a single product. Let's say you're producing a sophisticated piece of medical equipment. While the buttons and knobs and other lower-value parts in the machine could be made offshore, the advanced technology more likely must be fabricated here because of the skills gap between developing economies, like China, and the West.

But in general, comparative advantage does not favor one industry over another. It cleaves industries into discrete functions. And as network technology improves and overseas workers achieve higher education levels, more and more functions have the potential to be moved offshore.

The trouble with shifting comparative advantage is that it's sometimes hard to predict which jobs and businesses will be affected. As an advanced society, our bias favors education as a panacea. The more education we get, the more competitive we'll be. While more education is better than less, unfortunately, many jobs that require higher education will move offshore anyway, while other jobs that don't will remain here. The cabdriver can't be offshored. The housekeeper can't be offshored. The CPA's job can. The investment analyst's job can.

WHAT CAN WE DO?

If we can't readily educate ourselves out of this conundrum, how can we defend ourselves against shifting comparative advantage? Many in government and industry believe punitive economic measures are needed: raising tariffs and forcing currency reform. Both would produce unintended negative consequences.

The Currency Question

Many accuse China of keeping its exports artificially cheap by unfairly rigging its currency, the yuan. China pegged the yuan to the dollar in 1993, and when the dollar was strong, this seemed like a good idea to most. But as the dollar has fallen, many in the West believe that China's currency has become undervalued. This rigging, so the logic goes, is displacing jobs in the West. They insist that an appreciation in the value of China's currency will balance the trade gap and save U.S. and EU jobs. Congress has threatened to pass punitive sanctions on China, which would presume to wipe out the perceived currency advantage by levying huge tariffs on imports.

Serious economists differ on whether China's exchange rate is too low or too high, but even if the exchange rate is too low, it is only a minor contributor to the trade deficit between our two countries. If China and other Asian countries let their currencies appreciate by 20 percent, it would eliminate only one-fifth of the trade imbalance over the next few years, which is not nearly enough to bring the imbalance in line.

Actually, by keeping the yuan pegged to the weak dollar, China has been bankrolling America's spending for the last several years. China is America's second-largest lender after Japan. It has close to a trillion dollars in U.S. currency reserves, much of which is invested in U.S. Treasury bills. As the value of the dollar has slid, China has kept buying U.S. to shore up its savings. This has helped keep U.S. interest rates low.[4] If China's currency appreciates sharply in value, China would have less appetite for U.S. debt, which, it is widely believed, would trigger a rise in interest rates and a resulting slowdown of our economy.

A sharp revaluation of China's currency would also invite more speculators into an economy that is already awash in speculative capital. China wants to avoid that at all costs. The East Asian financial crisis walloped the economies of many neighboring countries, such as Thailand, Indonesia, and South Korea, and was caused in large part by the sudden departure of speculative capital from those economies.

Yet despite the economic risks, in the face of mounting pressure from the United States and the European Union, China recently allowed its currency to float within a narrow band against a basket of Asian currencies. Since then, China's currency has been appreciating in small increments. Considering that a sudden drastic swing in the value of the yuan could destabilize the economy, this pace seems prudent.

China has taken other less publicized steps to bring the trade balance in line. For example, they are rolling back export rebates. China exports used to be eligible for a rebate from the government on the value of the goods. This subsidy was put in place in the 1990s to stimulate export growth. However, China has reduced these rebates a couple times from their original 15 percent and has committed to the West to keep reducing the rebates over the next few years until they are eliminated. By rolling back export rebates, China is seeking to bring the currencies closer in line without tinkering with the exchange rate.

Protective Tariffs

In addition to pushing China to revalue its currency, many people advocate slapping high tariffs on Chinese imports. However, this action would harm American industries and our allies in Asia. Huge tariffs on apparel, for example, would restrain Chinese demand for American cotton. Huge tariffs on toys would check Chinese demand for American plastics. Huge tariffs on steel I-bars would soften Chinese demand for American iron ore.

Protective tariffs would also bite American affiliates in China. Today, over half of all the goods America imports from China come from *American affiliates in China.* That means, as U.S. imports from China swell, U.S. firms receive the lion's share of the profits. High tariffs would have the effect of shooting our own firms in the foot.

What's more, because of China's deep and unprecedented integration with its neighbors, punitive actions taken toward China, like restrictive trade barriers or tariffs, would have negative repercussions for the entire region. If you hit China, then China would be impelled to import less from its neighbors, including U.S. allies, which today are running huge surpluses with China: Taiwan at $57.9 billion; South Korea at $41.7 billion; Japan at $16.3 billion; and Australia at $5 billion.[5]

Trade is the best defense from Chinese direct investment and shifts in comparative advantage—more effective than protectionism or currency manipulations. By taking the fight to the Chinese, by building markets on the mainland, we ensure our piece of China's growing pie while helping to keep the region stable and prosperous.

IS TRADING WITH CHINA
AKIN TO ARMING A FUTURE ENEMY?

About half of all Americans believe that China's rise will be "a threat to world peace," and almost a third believe that China will "soon dominate the world," according to a Ipsos-Reid poll in April 2004.

Not surprisingly, then, I've heard many people tell me that doing business with China is nothing short of treason. But it's important to keep China's military modernization in perspective. The Chinese military of today is on a par with 1960s technology, weaponry, and command-and-control systems—it's a good fifty years behind the militaries of the West. Most analysts of the Chinese military believe it would take China until the end of this century before it's capable of effectively fighting even a moderate-sized military power. And with only twenty liquid fuel ICBMs, China lacks a credible first strike nuclear capability. It's dwarfed by the U.S. nuclear arsenal.

So, while China's defense spending has increased over the past years, this growth is very much in line with the natural path of a conventional military power—not the modernization program of a state seeking to become a military juggernaut or global superpower. In fact, many analysts believe that China is struggling to modernize its military more to advance its business interests than its military posture. For example, China is building a "blue water" navy in an effort to secure its shipping lanes in the Straits of Malacca and other key arteries of commerce, not for use in war, defense analysts argue.

The only major flashpoint is the issue of Taiwan. China is building up its forces across the Taiwan Strait, having deployed over 800 missiles so far and continuing at the rate of several dozen per year. Without a doubt, China could do more to help defuse tensions in cross-Strait relations. Reducing the number of missiles deployed and curtailing the chest-thumping rhetoric would go a long way to ratcheting down tensions.

Yet the simple fact remains that should China wish to take Taiwan by force, it has two rather unappealing choices: toppling the Taiwanese government, or military invasion. Either option would have devastating political and economic consequences for China.

China and Taiwan are deeply integrated economically. China buys more goods from Taiwan than from any other country in the world, save Japan. And its thirst for Taiwanese goods is growing at over 30 percent a year. Taiwan's demand for Chinese investments also has been pronounced. It's estimated that Taiwanese own over 100,000 businesses on the mainland. Hence, destabilizing Taiwan's leadership or invading would bring commerce between the two to a screeching halt, causing a crippling impact on the Chinese economy.

While many experts do not see China's push to modernize its military as a gambit to take Taiwan or achieve the global hegemony of a superpower, they do express concern for China's push to expand its economic influence around the world, or what some call China's "global charm offensive."

What's most noteworthy about China globe-trotting is its relative agnosticism toward ideology or political philosophy. China prefers not to interfere in the political affairs of its business partners. Instead,

China's Accumulated Outward FDI Flows, 1982–2002 (billions of dollars)

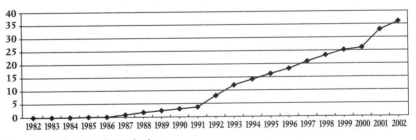

Source: UNCTAD, FDI/TNC database

Note: Data from 1985 to 1989 are from national sources. Data after 1989 are estimated by accumulating flows.

China cuts security agreements and trade deals with nations across every continent, in an effort to assure the markets and resources required to sustain its growth.

Although this trend may seem alarming, it's not new. China has pursued a steadily growing campaign of foreign direct investment (FDI) since the late 1970s.

Today, China invests an average of $2.3 billion a year in foreign countries, and that number is growing. About a third of China's companies investing overseas are large, state-owned enterprises such as China State Construction, China Chemicals Import and Export Corporation, and China Metals and Minerals Corporation. China's Asian neighbors have been the primary recipient of investment, followed by the United States and Africa.

In addition to direct investment, China also pursues other modes of engagement, such as trade and security agreements and cooperation on science and technology. Though many accuse China of cozying up to autocracies, such as Sudan and Burma, China also does business with many of America's allies around the world.

It's not a question of doing business with dictators. It's a question of doing business with *everybody*.

And that's the dynamic we've got to pay attention to. Although China's engagement across the globe helps to assure its continued integration into the international system, the trend also presents some strategic challenges to American interests. With China's increasing engagement comes increasing influence. As American prestige around the world ebbs to an all-time low, according to a recent Pew study, some polls show that China is generally regarded with esteem and trust.

Notably, though, there isn't a resulting desire to emulate the Chinese. In the 1980s during the boom of Japan's economy, many in the West actually wanted to *be* like the Japanese. A cottage industry sprang up teaching Western business executives how to run their corporations like Japanese managers. During the so-called China Century, however, few seem to want to be like China. And, save for the building of Confucian institutes around the world, China is not making much of a push to spread its culture and ideologies to other countries either. Rather, China prefers commerce to culture, yuan diplomacy to hard power.

To that end, China is going so far as to form its own multilateral organizations, such as the Shanghai Cooperation Organization. In the SCO, China is working with Russia and the oil-rich "Stans" on border security, joint military maneuvers, and pipeline and rail links—without the participation of the United States.

China's influence in the Middle East is also growing. China is the second-largest importer of oil in the world, and Saudi Arabia is China's number-one supplier, followed by Iran. China has therefore been able to secure some big oil deals, including one to allow a Chinese company to develop Iran's Yadavarn oil field in exchange for China's agreement to purchase Iranian liquefied natural gas. China's influence with the European Union is also on the rise, with a concerted, but failed, effort in 2005 to lift the EU arms embargo against China.

What can we do? China will keep trotting the globe doing deals, whether we hit them with tariffs or not. The only way to counter China's worldwide charm offensive is not to shut the Chinese out; it's to do business with them—*and to do business with their trading partners.* Thus, if you trade with Mexico, you'll be competing with China head-to-head. If you do business with Canada, you'll be taking on China economically. Vietnam, same thing. Doing business around the world counters China's spreading influence around the world.

And, by trading with the Chinese directly—by buying from them and selling to them—you'll not only be helping your bottom line, you'll also be helping to advance our policy and security goals in the region. As was the thinking behind the Marshall Plan, countries that are prosperous, stable, governed by the rule of law, and well integrated into the international community are less likely to go to war.

It is natural, since China and the United States compete for influence in Asia, that there will be some areas of contention. But this does not mean China is evil or our avowed enemy. Treating the Chinese as such will guarantee that they will be. But trading with China helps to keep the country on a path toward stability and modernity. Through doing business, we not only help to maintain America's primacy in the century ahead, but we also help to enhance our national security.

Afterword

SEEING THE FUTURE

From Beijing to Boca Raton

Our board meeting runs late again. Old business takes up all of the time allotted for new business. Now one director needs to make a plane for Dulles. We're left with our list of resolutions to approve. We intone the ayes and nays, a rushed catechism to bless the decisions of the day. The meeting is adjourned.

I'm sitting alone with my partner. We're looking at each other. We've both lost hair and put on weight.

"What'll you do now?" The board has signaled that we, the founders, are free to pursue other opportunities if we so desire—to let our CEO devote her full time to running the company. This dragon lady we hired from Accenture China a couple years ago has turned the joint around.

The goods today pass muster. "Good goods," as my grandfather used to say. They're compliant with customer and government requirements, and they arrive on time. The business is profitable again, and we're getting paid by our customers. We've also been able to climb the value chain a bit ourselves, specializing in more complex, engineered products now.

The dissident entrepreneur and I agree we'll still help out all we can to build our company's sales. Then he says he's going to do another

China deal. Get back to his investment banking routes. Something in telecom, perhaps.

Me? Well, I'll stick around a bit longer—at least until the original Miami guys get their money out. One ophthalmologist said to me the other day he hoped he'd see a return in his lifetime. I heartily agree with him.

We don't have a lifetime. To everything, there's a season. In the 1980s, Japan seemed on a flat trajectory to world economic dominance. But the business cycle prevailed, and Japan's harvest season was followed by a long season of sustained retrenchment.

China is not exempt from the laws of economics either. We are currently in a dynamic season of both reaping and sowing. But China's bumper crop won't last indefinitely. Nor can China continue to grow its GDP at the torrid rate of 10 percent a year without overheating.

We have a decade, maybe two, in which we can reap huge rewards from trading with China, and in so doing, influence what course China takes in world affairs. The Beijing Olympics presents an especially rare opportunity to do both.

LET THE GAMES BEGIN: THE BEIJING OLYMPICS '08

China is investing billions and billions of dollars in the Olympic Games. And that direct investment will ripple out into still more billions of dollars' worth of commerce. China wants to knock the world's socks off with its modernity at the Olympics. It wants to keep the spectators and athletes safe and the city orderly. And it wants to show everyone a terrific time. Each one of these avenues of Chinese investment presents big opportunities for Western firms.

To this end, the Beijing municipal government has thrown its doors open to foreign investment and participation in the various projects surrounding the Olympics. Several policies have been put in place to make the investment environment more hospitable: land is being priced below market value, ownership tendering of property after the games is being permitted, and the municipal government is providing foreign investors with risk support.

Over $2 billion is being spent on the venues for the games alone— including thirty-two sites in Beijing and five outside the city in Shanghai, Qingdao, and Tianjin. Almost half a billion dollars will be spent on constructing the Olympic village itself.

Aside from that, Beijing itself is getting a major makeover. The municipal government will invest about $24 billion in infrastructure alone in the run-up to the games: in transportation, airport construction, and wastewater treatment facilities.[1] In the works are 21 miles of new express rail, 65 miles of major roads, and 119 miles of railroad and subway lines to the airport and the Olympic village.

As for airport construction, they're building one new terminal, one new runway, and fifty-five aircraft parking aprons. Building equipment and supplies will be needed, plus air traffic management systems. Beijing has U.S. systems for monitoring and controlling air traffic and will be looking to purchase American equipment to carry out the requirements of the U.S. Federal Aviation Administration on safety and operations.

For wastewater treatment infrastructure, the government plans to build nine treatment plants, nine wastewater main pipelines (each one 630 miles long!), nine wastewater reclamation and reuse facilities, and four sludge-digesting facilities. The total investment is estimated to be $1.45 billion.

Also on the list are upgrades in technology infrastructure. Beijing will spend $3.6 billion on expanding fiber optic networks, augmenting the capacity of mobile communications networks, and putting in place a digital network that can transmit HDTV.

China is importing a tremendous amount of supplies, equipment, and services from the West to complete these large infrastructure projects. But aside from giving Beijing a makeover, China wants to keep its visitors safe. It's investing billions of dollars in security inside and outside of Beijing.

For one thing, the Chinese are trying to upgrade their emergency response systems in a hurry. China does not have a national technical standard for its systems, yet it's requiring all municipalities to install emergency response systems starting in 2006. The local governments are looking for solutions quickly. American firms have an advantage here, especially in data management systems and interoperability consoles. Airport security is another major avenue of investment, as Beijing increases its airport capacity for the games.

China also wants to show its guests a wonderful time. Over 1.5 million people are estimated to visit China during the games. They'll need places to stay and things to do. The hospitality, tourist, and entertainment industries will all get a big boost from the Olympics.*

The Olympics are not simply a golden opportunity to make money. They're a golden opportunity to help guide China's course in world affairs. Hosting an Olympics is no guarantee of good times ahead. The Sarajevo Olympics were thought to be a success until everyone turned inward and started killing one another.

Yet the eyes of the entire world will be upon China in 2008. This scrutiny will have a profound effect on how China behaves and will provide us with a glimpse of what China will become in the century ahead.

Of course, no one knows what kind of country China will turn out to be. Not the Tiananmen leaders, not even China's leaders. That's why American policy toward China is anchored on a paradox, pursuing two opposite strategies simultaneously: engage China, so that we can help guide what kind of country the most populous nation in the world will be, and hedge, in case China should emerge as a foe.

---

*For more information on Beijing Olympics 2008, visit AllTheT.com/olympics.

Many prefer to see only one side of the paradox—that China is a lethal foe. They see China's rise as an inevitable, woeful denouement to a century whose history has yet to be written. They've already named it the China Century. In other words, our goose is cooked.

Not so. The future will not be led by those who can make the cheapest copy of an auto part. Innovation, not imitation, will lead the next century. Advances in medical technology and biotechnology, aerospace, oceanography, agricultural science, and information systems, environmental and energy technology—these areas of inquiry will lead the next century, and they're sweet spots of American science and industry.

The extent to which China continues to be a closed system, restricting the free flow of information, people, and capital, will determine whether China will be a follower or a leader in the century ahead.

But the jinni has been loosed from the bottle. The Chinese people have glimpsed the possibility of a better tomorrow, and they want it for themselves and for their kids. China's leaders, schooled in history, see the regime as a short blip on the long timeline of China's path to modernity. Their very survival rests on whether they can add a billion people to the world's modern middle class.

I wish they'd hurry. My people are impatient.

ACKNOWLEDGMENTS

And I thought doing business in China was hard. A squalid little factory in the provinces is a lot friendlier than an empty page. This book could not have been written without the help of family, friends, and mentors.

Thanks in particular to Joy Drucker, my bride to be, for her bottomless wellspring of support, inspiration, and editing. My compulsion for rewrites was topped only by her compulsion for rereads.

Thanks also to my family. When they weren't asking me every eleven minutes if the book was finished yet, their patience and optimism were unflagging. Thanks to Richard, Adam, and Hilary Haft, and Joy and Arthur Gillman.

Thanks also to Jon Mozes, who set me on this journey and never quit my side. To Stephanie Ansin, Gary Eisenberg, Scott Heiferman, Gerald W. Moore, David Rheins, Glen Roberts, Lisa Shields, Wick Sloan, Andrew Susman, and Feng Wang, I thank you for your contributions, wisdom, and help along the way.

I'd also like to thank Kate Rosow, who was magically able to coax data out of a country where accurate information is scarce. Her research contribution to the book was invaluable.

To my teachers—Dan Bowden, Mike Stokes, and Ted Tayler—you have my lifelong gratitude.

To my mentors and colleagues, I also give my deepest thanks and appreciation. Thanks in particular to Jeff Bader, Charles W. Freeman III, Kerry Dumbaugh, Hani Findakly, Mark Fung, Charles Ludolph,

Dan Spiegel, Bill Reinsch, Eric Biel, Marjorie Kalter, Arlene Fromberg, Paul Dawson, Monty Cerf, Don Deglau, Anthony Cino, Molly Wilkinson, Kristina Svensson, and Sam Cheow.

A special thanks also to my agent, Susan Golomb, whose brains and moxie made this project possible. And to the superb team at Portfolio—Adrian Zackheim, Branda Maholtz, and Will Weisser, in particular—I give you my deepest thanks.

NOTES

Chapter 1: Getting Started

1. U.S. International Trade Commission, U.S. Department of Commerce.
2. Ibid.
3. Ibid., "The Role of Small and Medium Sized Enterprises in Exports to China: A Statistical Profile," December 2005.
4. Jeffrey A. Bader, "China's Emergence and Its Implications for the United States" (presentation to the Brookings Council, Washington, D.C., February 14, 2006).
5. Elizabeth Economy, "China's Environmental Challenge" (testimony before the U.S.-China Economic and Security Review Commission Hearing on Major Challenges Facing the Chinese Leadership, February 2, 2006), p. 3.
6. "Behind the Mask," *Economist,* March 18, 2004.
7. Ibid.
8. Thomas Lun, "Social Unrest in China," Congressional Research Service, May 8, 2006, p. 1.
9. "Behind the Mask."
10. Ibid.
11. World Bank.
12. "China's Environment: A Great Wall of Waste," *Economist,* August 19, 2004.
13. Elizabeth Economy, *The River Runs Black: The Environmental Challenge to China's Future* (Ithaca, N.Y.: Cornell University Press, 2004).
14. Ambassador Charles W. Freeman Jr., USFS (Ret.), "The Arabs Take a Chinese Wife: Sino-Arab Relations in the Decade to Come" (remarks to the World Affairs Council of Northern California at Asilomar), May 7, 2006.
15. David Barboza, "China Drafts Law to Empower Unions and End Labor Abuse," *New York Times,* October 13, 2006.
16. Thomas Kun and Dick Nanto, "China's Trade with the United States and the World," Congressional Research Service, January 23, 2006; http://www.fas.org/sgp/crs/row/RL31403.pdf.

Chapter 2: Reading the Market

1. "China Overtakes U.S. as Investment Target," *USA Today Online,* June 28, 2004.
2. Bader, "China's Emergence."

3. U.S. Department of State. *U.S. Committed to Making Trade with China Fair,* April 21, 2004.

4. *USTR Says* (USTR fact sheet); http://usinfo.state.gov/eap/Archive/2004/Jul/02-962878.html.

5. William Ward, "Manufacturing Productivity and the Shifting US, China and Global Job Scenes—1990 to 2005," Clemson University Center for International Trade Working Paper 052507, August 2005.

6. Based on the top 10 percent of China's earners: PPP of 14k per annum, based on data from World Bank, China Population Information Network, and CEIC data, December 2004.

7. Jon Hilsenrath and Rebecca Buckman, "Factory Employment Is Falling World-Wide" *Wall Street Journal Online,* October 20, 2003.

8. Ibid.

9. For more statistics, visit U.S. Office of Textiles and Apparel online.

10. Anne Marie Squeo, "Safe Harbor: How Longshoremen Keep Global Wind at Their Backs," *Wall Street Journal Online,* July 26, 2006.

11. James Miller, "Lockout Shutters West Coast Ports; Activities Halted through Sunday," *Chicago Tribune,* September 28, 2002.

12. China National Bureau of Statistics, January 24, 2006.

Chapter 3: Orienting Yourself

1. Kate Xiao Zhao, *How the Farmers Changed China* (Boulder, Colo.: Westview Press, 1996), 106.

2. John McMillan and Christopher Woodruff, "The Central Role of Entrepreneurs in Transition Economies," *The Journal of Economic Perspectives* 16, no. 3 (2002).

3. "Are You Being Served? China's Service Sector Is Escaping from the Shadow of Manufacturing, but Not as Fast as It Could," *Economist,* January 12, 2006.

4. Bill Powell, "Uncharted Waters: When CNOOC's CEO Set His Sights on Unocal, He Had No Idea of the Storm He'd Cause in D.C. and His Boardroom," *Time,* Asia ed., July 11, 2005.

5. C. Fred Bergsten, Bates Gill, Nicholas Lardy, and Derek Mitchell, *China: The Balance Sheet; What the World Needs to Know Now About the Emerging Superpower* (Public Affairs, 2006), 38.

Chapter 4: Buying from China

1. Leo Hindery Jr., "Wal-Mart's Giant Sucking Sound," *Business Week Online,* October 7, 2005.

2. Jamie Bolton and Wenbo Liu, "Fulfillment Excellence in Today's China," *Accenture,* 2006, p. 6.

3. Diana Huang and Mark Kader, "Third-Party Logistics in China: Still a Tough Market," Mercer Management Consulting, *Mercer on Travel and Transport,* 2002.

4. For more city information, visit buyusa.gov, tdctrade.com (the trade Web site for Hong Kong), and individual cities' Web sites.

Chapter 5: Selling to China

1. For more specific information on policies, statistics, laws, and regulations, see the official Web site of the Ministry of Commerce of the People's Republic of China, english.mofcom.gov.cn.
2. David Menzie, Pui-Kwan Tse, Mike Fenton, "China's Growing Appetite for Minerals," U.S. Geological Survey Open-File Report 2004-1374, 2004, http://pubs.usgs.gov/of/2004/1374/.
3. Amy Raskin and Brad Lindenbaum, "China: Is the World Really Prepared?" *Bernstein Investment Research and Planning,* December 2004.
4. Interviews with company management.
5. "Are You Being Served?"
6. "Foreign Insurers in China: Opportunity and Risk," KPMG and Reuters, 2005.
7. For more specific information on policies, laws, and regulations for foreign insurance firms in China, see the official Web site of the China Insurance Regulatory Commission (CIRC), http://61.135.237.6/Portal45/default2727.htm.
8. Brent Evans, "Math Professor Helping Shape China's Insurance Industry," *Advanced on the Web,* March 11, 2002.
9. Matthew Gettman and Stephanie Decker, "A Guide to Doing Business in China and Information on Current Economic Conditions," U.S. Commercial Service and U.S. Department of State, 2004.
10. For more statistics, visit the General Administration of Customs of the People's Republic of China's Web site at http://english.customs.gov.cn/default.aspx.
11. "US Ag Export Outlook: China Moves Ahead of EU To Take 4th Position," Cattlenetwork.com online, May 25, 2006.
12. "China Doubling Coal Mine Shutdowns," CNN.com, November 7, 2006.
13. "More Shipbuilding Giants to Tap HK Equity Market," Chinadaily.com, November 15, 2006.
14. Bella Thomas, "What the World's Poor Watch on TV," *Prospect Magazine* 82 (January 2003).
15. Rone Tempest and Maggie Farley, "China Slams Door on Direct-Sales Firms," *Los Angeles Times,* April 24, 1998.
16. According to the U.S. Commercial Sales brief on direct sales, available at www.buyusainfo.net/docs/x_5677683.pdf.

Chapter 6: Competing with China

1. *Mergers and Acquisitions,* February 2006.
2. *Washington Post,* July 3, 2005.
3. Joint CIPA/World Bank Group Workshop on China's Outward Forward Direct Investment, Beijing, China, June 13, 2006.

4. Bergsten et al., *China: The Balance Sheet*, 108.

5. "China's Trade with the United States and the World," Congressional Research Service, March 14, 2006.

Afterword: Seeing the Future

1. Tom Van Riper, "Host City Curse," *Forbes.com*, February 8, 2006.

INDEX

adjacent markets, entry into, 82

advertising agencies
    market prospects, 118
    using large versus local, 149

advertising media, 97, 149–50

after-sales support
    potential competition and, 174
    prohibition of, 154

agents for distribution, 136–37

agricultural industries
    chemical product testing and quotas,
        122–23
    cities specializing in, 76, 78, 79, 80
    market prospects, 120, 122–23
    restrictions and prohibitions, 140, 146
    U.S. trade representatives for, 122

aircraft parts, Chinese importation of, 80

airport security opportunities, 129–30, 190

air traffic management (ATM) equipment
    opportunities, 123, 189

Alibaba.com, 91

America. See United States

Amway, 151

animal husbandry industries restrictions
    and prohibitions, 121, 140, 146

apparel industry
    circular trade, 28–29
    cities specializing in, 76, 78
    number of Chinese manufacturers, 173

arms embargo, 8, 120

arts and culture industry restrictions, 145

ATM (air traffic management) equipment
    opportunities, 123, 189

automotive industries
    cities specializing in, 77, 78, 79, 124
    emissions standards, 129
    market prospects, 13, 124–25, 131
    number of Chinese manufacturers, 173
    tariffs, 153

Avon, 150

back-door sales, 159, 160, 162

backup suppliers, 39

balance of trade. See also two-way trade
    currency reform, 178–80
    shift in, 20
    tariffs, 29, 180

bank cards, market prospects for, 127–28

bankers, international, 93

bank financing and support, 93

banking and finance industries
    market prospects, 126–27
    restrictions and prohibitions, 144–45,
        147

beer and wine industries
    market prospects, 120–21
    in Qingdao, 78
    restrictions, 141

Beijing, 128–29, 134, 188–90

biotechnology, cities specializing in, 77,
    79

boards of directors, 46–47

boatbuilding industries
    cities specializing in, 76, 78
    market prospects, 131

bovine products restrictions, 121
B&Q (do-it-yourself retailer), 115
brand building, 113–14
brand loyalty, potential competition and,
   173
British Petroleum, 168
Buffet, Warren, 116
Buick, 114
building materials, cities specializing in, 75,
   77, 78, 79, 80. See also steel industry
Bush, George H. W., 8, 168
business cards, exchange of, 59–60

capitalism in China, 39–41
cash-to-cash cycle, management of, 98
Caterpillar, 126
Cavalier Homes, 83–85
Center for Automotive Research, 29
CFIUS (Committee on Foreign
   Investment in the United States),
   167–68
Changhong Electronics Group, 171
chemical industries
   agricultural, market prospects and
      restrictions, 122–23
   chemical fiber production restrictions,
      141–42
   cities specializing in, 75, 76, 77, 78, 79,
      80
   specialty chemicals, Chinese imports
      of, 111
   tariffs, 153
Chengdu, features and key industries of,
   75–76
Chery, 124
child hunger in China, 11
China. See also United States and China,
   differences between; specific issues
   and industries
   as American market opportunity, 2, 5,
      12–13, 21, 110–14

business environment, 13–15
   corruption and fraud, 7
   environmental issues, 11–13, 128–29
   geography and demography, 9
   global influence, 182–84
   political economy, 9–11
   regional trading partners, 19–20
   and United States, complementary
      economies of, 20, 28
China Association of Automobile
   Manufacturers, 124
China Mobile, 133–34
China National Offshore Oil Corporation
   (CNOOC), 47
China Unicom, 133–34
Chum King, LLC, 86–88
CIF (cost, insurance, and freight
   included) quotations, 92
circular trade, 28–31
CIT (financial services firm), 94
Citgo, 168
cities, key industries in, 75–80
clothing. See apparel industry
CNOOC (China National Offshore Oil
   Corporation), 47
coal mining equipment, market prospects
   for, 125–26
College Comfort, LLC, 96–97
commercial terms, 94–96
Committee on Foreign Investment in the
   United States (CFIUS), 167–68
communication, face-to-face
   to evaluate creditworthiness, 115
   at trade fairs, 75, 80
   in trust-building, 53, 56–57
communication failures. See also cultural
   issues
   differences in logic and rhetoric, 43–44
   differences in standards, 73–75
   lack of analogous concepts, 45–51, 163
   recognition of differences, 32–34
comparative advantage, shift of, 176–80

competition from China
  back-door sales, 159, 160, 162
  currency valuation and, 178–80
  direct investment in U.S., 166, 169–72,
    182–83
  job creation and, 165, 171
  low price points, 85–86
  monitoring of markets for, 172–74
  protective tariffs and, 29, 180
  shifting comparative advantage, 176–78
computers. *See* information technology
    (IT) industries; Internet
computer software industry
  market prospects, 133
  in Nanjing, 77
confidentiality agreements, 175–76
construction boom, 18–19, 189
construction industries
  equipment, market prospects for, 126
  materials, cities specializing in, 75, 77,
    78, 79, 80
  number of Chinese equipment
    manufacturers, 173
consulting services, opportunity for, 170
consumer base in China
  consumer education, 112, 116, 118–19
  customer service and after-sales
    support, 154
  demand for goods and services, 2, 21
  importation of products for, 111
  materialism, 113–14
  price-consciousness, 151
contingency backup suppliers, 39
contractual rights and obligations
  absence of Chinese concept for, 49–50
  purchase order for clarification of,
    94–95
controlling interest, definition of, 169–70
corporate forms in China, 137–40
corporate taxes, 154
corporation law
  confidentiality agreements, 175

contractual rights and obligations,
    49–50
  fiduciary duty, 45–48
  intellectual property, 160–64
  representations and warranties, 50–51
cosmetics industries
  intellectual property, 160–61
  tariffs, 153
cost, insurance, and freight included
    (CIF) quotations, 92
cost, total delivered
  direct labor, 73–74, 80–81
  fragmentation of industries and, 67–69
  leanness of business and, 88–89
  miscalculations, 66
  start-up costs, 81
  transportation of goods, 69–70, 81
cost modeling, 90
credit cards, market prospects for, 127–28
credit information and support, 114–15
cultural issues
  brand and fashion concepts, 113–14
  Chinese name conventions, 62–63
  eating and drinking, 61–62
  exchange of business cards, 59–60
  face, concept of, 58–59
  guanxi, 53
  laughter, 60–61
  legal concepts, 45–51, 163
  logic and rhetoric, 43–44
  manners and formality, 59
  negotiation style, 57–58
  sales pitch tips, 154–55
  use of time, 56–57
currency reform, 178–80
customs brokers, 91–92
customs valuation, 153

Dairy Queen, 112, 148
Dalian, 76, 132, 134
data management opportunities, 190

defective merchandise. *See* quality control
defense industries regulations and
    prohibitions, 8, 120, 147, 151
Deloitte & Touche, 118
Deng Xiaoping, 7, 9, 39–40, 113–14
development zones, 110, 152
direct foreign investment, Chinese, 166,
    169–72, 182–83
direct selling in China, 150–51
dissident entrepreneurs, 1–2, 5–9, 11, 17
distribution
    fragmentation in, 67–68, 115
    use of agents or distributors, 136–37
documents
    bookkeeping and fiduciary duty, 45–46
    filing of, 105–7
    purchase orders, 64–96
    for quality and procedural control, 48
    quality control of, 104
    templates for, 105–6
    types of, 99–104
draft payment, 95
dual use products, 120
Dubai Ports World, 165–66
due diligence, 89–91
Duratek, Inc., 13

eating and drinking as cultural issue,
    61–62
economic and technology development
    zones, 110, 152
economic considerations in import
    program, 80–81, 110
education and training, competitiveness
    and, 178
education and training industries, 128,
    145
education of consumers, 112, 116, 118–19
e-learning systems, 128
electrical machinery export to China, 111
electronics industries

cities specializing in, 76, 77, 78, 79, 80
    restrictions, 143
emergency backup suppliers, 39
employment. *See* labor
energy policy, Chinese, 12
energy-related industries
    cities specializing in, 77, 79
    environmental protection initiatives,
        129
    growth in American export to China,
        111
    market prospects, 125–26, 132–33
    restrictions and prohibitions, 143, 147
engineering terms, 96
entrepreneurialism in China, 39–41
environmental challenges, Chinese,
    11–13, 128–29
equipment manufacturing industry
    restrictions, 143
Ericsson, 168
European Standard II on automobile
    emissions, 129
expectations, lowering of, 56–57
Export-Import Bank of the United States,
    94
export rebates, 179–80
extension of core business lines, 83–85

face concept
    in Chinese business customs, 58–59
    Chinese name conventions, 62–63
    eating and drinking, 61–62
    exchange of business cards, 59–60
    laughter, 60–61
face-to-face communication
    to evaluate creditworthiness, 115
    at trade fairs, 75, 80
    in trust-building, 53, 56–57
factors, financing by, 93
farming industries. *See* agricultural
    industries; animal husbandry

industries restrictions and
prohibitions
FDI (foreign direct investment), Chinese,
166, 169–72, 182–83
FedEx, 70, 79
fiduciary duty, 45–48
finance and banking industries
market prospects, 126–27
restrictions and prohibitions, 144–45,
147
financial reports. *See* documents
financing of import program, 93–94
fishery industries
cities specializing in, 76
market prospects, 131–32
restrictions and prohibitions, 140, 146
fish meal, market prospects for, 121
flat worldview of economics, 25–32
FOB (free on board vessel) quotations,
92
food and beverage industries
cities specializing in, 75, 76, 77, 78, 79,
80
FDA regulations, 42
market prospects, 120–22
restrictions and prohibitions, 141, 146
tariffs, 153
Foreign Commercial Service, Gold Key
program, 135
foreign direct investment (FDI), Chinese,
166, 169–72, 182–83
forestry industries restrictions and
prohibitions, 140, 146
fragmentation in Chinese industry, 67–70,
114, 115
franchising, 129, 148
free on board vessel (FOB) quotations, 92
freight forwarders, 91–92, 105
fruits
cities specializing in, 76
market prospects, 121–22
Fujian Province (Xiamen), 79–80, 132

gaming, online and mobile, market
prospects for, 134
garments. *See* apparel industry
GDP (gross domestic product), China's,
10, 19, 31, 41, 116–17, 128, 188
General Electric, 76, 171
Germany, 27
glass industry in Wuhan, 79
Glenoit Corp Specialty Fabrics, 168
goals of business
defense of price points, 85–86
entry into new or adjacent markets,
82–83
extension of core business lines,
83–85
launch of new business, 86–89
Gold Key program, Foreign Commercial
Service, 135
Gould, Stephen Jay, 25–26
governmental resources, 94, 135
government procurement in China, 151
grain. *See* agricultural industries
green products and services, market
prospects for, 12–13, 128–29
gross domestic product (GDP), China's,
10, 19, 31, 41, 116–17, 128, 188
Guangdong Province (Shenzhen), 78–79,
132
Guangzhou, as port city, 132
guanxi, 53

Haft, Jeremy
business model, 37–38
failed ventures, 158–59
first venture in China, 41–43
legal issues at inception of business,
175–76
plastics resin venture, 1, 4–5, 15, 23–24,
34–35, 109–10
reliance on industry consultant, 107–8,
187

Haier Group, 170–71

Hangzhou, features and key industries of, 76

Harbin, features and key industries of, 76–77

heavy machinery industry in Wuhan, 79

Henry Schein, Inc., 48, 161

household goods, cities specializing in, 76, 77

Huawei Electronics, 115, 172

Huayi Group, 168

Hubei Province (Wuhan), features and key industries of, 79

IBM, 76, 79, 168

IFC (International Finance Corporation), 115

import program, feasibility of
Chinese industrial capabilities and, 73–80
for defense of price points from competition, 85–86
economic considerations, 80–81
for entry into adjacent markets, 82–83
for extension of core business lines, 83–85
for launch of new business, 86–89

import program, management of
buying commitments, 96–97
customs broker, use of, 91–92
due diligence, 89–91
financing, 93–94
shipping, 105–7
terms, clarification of, 94–96
vigilance, 97–105

India, 20, 25, 40

industrial cities in China, 75–80

information flow, restriction of, 162

information management, 99–104

information technology (IT) industries
cities specializing in, 75, 76, 77
market prospects, 127

insourcing, 170–71

inspection report template, 105, 106

insurance industries
market penetration and prospects, 117–18
restrictions, 117, 144–45

intellectual property, 160–64, 175–76

intermediaries. See middlemen

international bankers, 93

International Finance Corporation (IFC), 115

international law firms, 51, 53, 114

International Ship and Port Security Codes (ISPS), 132

International Trade Administration, U.S. Department of Commerce, 135

Internet
for advertising, 150
in Chinese factories, 25
gaming, market prospects for, 134
middlemen, 91
projected use in China, 133
role in Tiananmen Square uprising, 6
in U.S. businesses, 25

Ipsos-Reid poll, 181

iron industries, cities specializing in, 78–79

iron ore, Chinese importation of, 111

ISPS (International Ship and Port Security Codes), 132

IT. See information technology (IT) industries

Japan, 19, 27

Jiangsu Province (Nanjing), features and key industries of, 77

jobs. See labor

joint ventures (JV), 138–39

KFC, 129
Konka Electronics, 171
Korea, 19

labor
  circles of trade and, 29–31
  conditions, 12
  cost of, 73–74, 75, 80–81
  job creation, 4, 165, 171
  job loss, 10, 26–28, 160
  migrant workers, 10
  skilled, 70–71, 75, 159–60
  work ethic, 71
law firms, international, 51, 53, 114
leather ass, 57
legal concepts
  confidentiality agreements, 175
  contractual rights and obligations,
    49–50
  fiduciary duty, 45–48
  intellectual property, 160–64
  representations and warranties, 50–51
legal services
  market prospects, 119
  restrictions, 145
  use of international law firms, 51, 53,
    114
Lego, 164
Lenovo, 115, 168
letters of credit, 95–96
licensing of technology, 148–49
liquefied natural gas equipment, market
  prospects for, 132
listening strategically, 54–55
livestock and livestock products, market
  prospects for, 121
logic and rhetoric in Chinese culture,
  43–44
logistics, management of, 69–70, 91–92
logistics companies, financing by, 94
low price points, defense of, 85–86

machinery manufacturing industries
  cities specializing in, 75, 76, 77, 78, 79,
    80
  market prospects, 131
  restrictions, 143
Malaysia, 20
manners
  business cards, 59–60
  Chinese names, 62–63
  eating and drinking, 61–62
  face concept and, 58–59
  formality, 59
  laughter, 60–61
  sales pitch tips, 154–55
manufacturers in China, strengths of,
  70–71
manufacturing industries restrictions and
  prohibitions, 141–43, 146–47
marine industries. See fishery industries
markets, new. See also specific industries
  adjacent markets, entry into, 82
  building of, 112–14
  detection of, 34
  extension of core business lines, 83–85
  governmental assistance, 94, 122, 135
  launch of new business, 86–89
  sales pitch tips, 154–55
  selection of, 115–20
McDonald's, 79, 129
medical product and equipment
    industries. See also pharmaceuticals
  market prospects, 135
  restrictions and prohibitions, 142, 146
  in Shenzhen, 78
medical treatment business restrictions,
  145
metallurgy
  cities specializing in, 75, 77, 78, 79
  restrictions and prohibitions, 143, 147
metals, Chinese importation of, 111
middle class, Chinese
  consumer education, 112

middle class, Chinese *(cont.)*
  demand for goods and services, 2, 21
  expansion of, 2, 19
  materialism, 113–14
  per capita income and wage growth,
    112–13
middlemen
  advantages and drawbacks in use of,
    88–89
  fragmentation of supply and
    distribution chains, 67–69, 84–85
  Internet, 91
  monitoring of, 97
military industries regulations and
  prohibitions, 8, 120, 147, 151
mining and quarrying industries
  restrictions and prohibitions, 141,
    146
miscommunication. *See also* cultural
  issues
  differences in logic and rhetoric, 43–44
  differences in standards, 73–75
  lack of analogous concepts, 45–51,
    163
  recognition of differences, 32–34
mobile communications
  for Beijing Olympics, 189
  market prospects, 133–34
  number of Chinese manufacturers, 173
Moltech Power Systems, 168
most-favored-nation status, 152
Multi-Fiber Agreement, 28

Nanjing, features and key industries of,
  77
national security, trade with China and, 4,
  166, 181, 184–85
natural gas equipment, market prospects
  for, 132
net payment terms, 94
New Balance, 164

Ningbo
  description of, 18
  features and key industries, 22, 77
  Plastics City, 23–24
  as port city, 18, 77, 132
Nokia, 168
nontradable industries, 177

objectives of business
  defense of price points, 85–86
  entry into new or adjacent markets,
    82–83
  extension of core business lines, 83–85
  launch of new business, 86–89
oil, Chinese importation of, 111, 184
Olympics, 188–90
one-child policy, 9
open accounts, 94
Opium Wars, 52

Pacific Life, 94
packaging industry in Wuhan, 79
paper making industry in Ningbo, 77
payment terms, 94–96
People's Bank of China, 127
People's Liberation Army (PLA), 8
per inquiry advertising arrangements,
  97
petrochemicals, cities specializing in, 76,
  77, 78, 79
petroleum processing and coking
  industries restrictions, 141
pharmaceuticals
  cities specializing in, 75, 76, 78, 80
  number of Chinese manufacturers, 173
  restrictions and prohibitions, 142,
    146–47
Philippines, 20
photo electronics industry in Wuhan, 79
PLA (People's Liberation Army), 8

plastics industries
  cities specializing in, 23, 78, 79, 80
  FDA regulations, 42
  recycled resins, Chinese importation
    of, 110
pleasure boats, market prospects for, 131
PO (purchase orders), 94–95
ports
  Chinese, 132
  in U.S. under foreign control, 165–66
poultry and poultry products, market
    prospects for, 121
power supply industries
  cities specializing in, 77, 79
  environmental protection initiatives, 129
  growth in American export to China,
    111
  market prospects, 125–26, 132–33
  restrictions and prohibitions, 143, 147
PPP (purchasing power parity), 32
precision instrument industry in Nanjing,
    77
prepayment for production, 96
price points, defense of, 85–86
price quotations, 89–90, 92
price segmentation, potential
    competition and, 174
pricing strategy, 151–54
printing industry, 79, 141
print media advertising, 149–50
product life, potential competition and,
    173
profitability, monitoring of, 107
profit margins
  as leverage, 90–91
  potential competition and, 173
prohibited foreign investment in China,
    146–47
protective tariffs, 29, 180
public facility service industries
    restrictions, 145
public health industries restrictions, 145

purchase orders (PO), 94–96
purchasing power parity (PPP), 32

Qingdao, 77–78, 132, 189
quality control
  active management of factories, 71–72
  defect rate, monitoring of, 107
  of documents, 104, 105
  engineering and regulatory terms, 96
  export of raw materials to China, 110
  fragmentation of manufacturing and, 69
  inspection report template, 105, 106
  procedural documentation for, 48
  samples, evaluation of, 91
  standards, differences in, 73–75
  standards, noncompliance with, 42–43,
    55, 65
  third-party quality assurance labs, 48
  tolerance for defective units, 87
quarrying and mining industries
    restrictions, 141
quotas on Chinese importation of
    fertilizers, 123

rail system in China, 69–70
raw materials, exportation of
  China as market for, 110–11
  circular trade, 29
  quality control and, 48, 110
  tariff and tax considerations, 110, 152,
    180
real estate industries restrictions, 145
recreational boats, market prospects for,
    131
regulation compliance. See quality
    control
regulations, Chinese. See also specific
    industries
  complexity of, 67, 70, 114–15
  for direct selling, 150

regulations, Chinese (*cont.*)
  prohibited foreign investment, 146–47
  restricted foreign investment, 140–46
reintermediation, 160–61
representations and warranties, 50–51
representative offices in China, 138
research industries restrictions, 145
restricted foreign investment in China, 140–46
risk tolerance, 80
Royal Dutch Shell, 168
rubber products industries restrictions, 143
Ryder Systems, 34, 70

schedules and timetables, 56–57
Schein, Inc., 48, 161
scientific research industries restrictions, 145
SCO (Shanghai Cooperation Organization), 184
Securitas, 168
security, national, trade with China and, 4, 166, 181, 184–85
security and safety industries, market prospects for, 129–30, 190
segmented markets, potential competition and, 174
semiconductor industry, market prospects for, 130
sensitive industries restrictions, 8, 120, 140–48, 151
services, Chinese need for, 2, 21, 29, 116–20, 170. *See also specific industries*
Shandong Province (Qingdao), 77–78, 132, 189
Shanghai
  manufacturing specialties, 22, 124
  Olympic site, 189
  as port city, 18, 132
  water shortage, 134

Shanghai Cooperation Organization (SCO), 184
Shanghai Haixin Group, 168
Shenzhen, 78–79, 132
shifting comparative advantage, 176–80
shipbuilding
  cities specializing in, 76, 78
  market prospects, 131
shipping
  document flow, 105–7
  in evaluation of import program, 81
  export licenses, 140
  freight forwarders and customs brokers, 91–92
  intra-China transportation of goods, 69–70
  U.S. to China, costs of, 110
Sichuan Province (Chengdu), features and key industries of, 75–76
sight draft payment, 95
Singapore, 20
Skyworth, 171
small and medium-sized enterprises (SMEs), 2–3
social service industries restrictions, 145
Sodexho USA, 168
software industry
  market prospects, 133
  in Nanjing, 77
Sony, 79, 164
sourcing firms, 82–83, 85–86, 87
special economic and technology development zones, 152
specifications. *See* quality control
sports industries restrictions, 145
standards. *See* quality control
Standards Group (advertising agency), 118–19
start-up costs, 81
steel industry
  cities specializing in, 77, 78, 79, 80
  market prospects, 13, 111

number of Chinese manufacturers, 173
    tariffs, 153
suppliers, appraisal of, 91
supply chain, fragmentation and
    middlemen in, 66–70, 84–85
Sweden, 27

Taiwan, 19, 181–82
tariffs
    economic and technology
        development zones, 110, 152
    in pricing strategy, 152–53
    protective, 29, 180
taxes
    in economic and technology
        development zones, 110, 152
    value-added and corporate, 153–54
TCL, 115, 172
technology
    for banking, market prospects for,
        126–27
    biotech, cities specializing in, 77, 79
    information technology, 75, 76, 77, 127
    infrastructure for, 189
    licensing of, 148–49
    for military and government
        applications, 151
    technology development zones, 152
telecommunications industries
    market prospects, 133–34
    restrictions, 143–44
television advertising, 97, 149
test-marketing, 97
textile industry
    cities specializing in, 76, 78, 79, 80
    restrictions, 141
Thailand, 20
third-party logistics providers (3PL), 70
third-party quality assurance labs, 48, 91
3Com, 172
3 L's in negotiations, 54–58

3PL (third-party logistics providers), 70
Tiananmen dissident entrepreneurs, 1–2,
    5–9, 11, 17
Tianjin, 79, 132, 189
timeline management, 105, 107
timetables and schedules, 56–57
tin, Chinese importation of, 111
tobacco processing industry restrictions,
    141
tolerances. *See* quality control
tolling businesses, 110
total delivered cost
    direct labor, 73–74, 80–81
    fragmentation of industries, 67–69
    leanness of business and, 88–89
    miscalculations, 66
    start-up costs, 81
    transportation of goods, 69–70, 81
town and village enterprise (TVE), 41
tradable industries, 177
trade fairs, 75, 80
trade industries, wholesale and retail,
    restrictions on, 144
trade representatives for agricultural
    products, 122
trade secrets, 160–64, 175–76
training and education, competitiveness
    and, 178
training and education industries, market
    prospects for, 128
transportation equipment industries,
    cities specializing in, 76, 78
transportation of goods, intra-China,
    69–70
transportation services restrictions, 143–44
triangular debt, 51
trucking, intra-China, 70
trust building
    Chinese names, correct use of, 62–63
    Chinese wariness of foreigners, 52–53
    eating and drinking customs, 61–62
    exchange of business cards, 59–60

trust building *(cont.)*
   face concept, 58–59
   face-to-face communication, 53, 56–57
   laughter, avoidance of, 60–61
   in penetration of Chinese markets, 137
   3 L's, 54–58
Tsingtao beer, 120
TV advertising, 97, 149
TVE (town and village enterprise), 41
two-way trade
   in apparel industry, 28–29
   in Asian countries, 19–20
   benefits to labor, 4, 29–31
   circular trade, 28–31
   to parry Chinese competition, 3–4
   for tax advantage and quality control,
      110

unemployment, 10, 26–28, 160
UNICEF, 11
unions, 12, 29–31
United Kingdom, 26
United States. *See also specific issues and*
      industries
   and China, complementary economies
      of, 20, 28
   Chinese direct investment in, 166,
      169–72, 182–83
   failing industries and job losses, 13,
      26–27
   market opportunities in China, 2, 5,
      12–13, 21, 110–14
United States and China, differences
      between
   face concept, 58–63
   legal concepts, 45–51, 163
   logic and rhetoric, 43–44
   recognition of, 32–34
   sales pitch tips, 154–55
   standards, 73–75
University of Connecticut, 118

UPS, 70, 94
U.S. Department of Agriculture, 122
U.S. Department of Commerce, 122, 135,
      151
U.S. Office of Textiles and Apparel, 28
U.S. State Department Office of Defense
      Trade, 151
U.S. trade representatives for agricultural
      products, 122

value-added taxes (VAT), 153–54
value proposition, 80
virtuous circle of trade, 28–31
Volkswagen, 23

Wal-Mart, 12, 48–49, 66, 79, 89
Walton, Sam, 66
water and wastewater treatment, market
      prospects for, 134–35, 189
weapons industries regulations and
      prohibitions, 8, 120, 147, 151
wholly owned foreign enterprises
      (WOFE), 139–40
wine and beer industries
   market prospects, 120–21
   in Qingdao, 78
   restrictions, 141
workers. *See* labor
work ethic, 71
World Bank, 112–13, 170
World Trade Organization (WTO), 19,
      126
Wuhan, features and key industries of, 79

Xiamen, 79–80, 132

Zhejiang Province (Hangzhou), features
      and key industries of, 76